THE PHONE RANG . . .

It was Lymie, all excited. "Tyler, they found our heads! You should have seen it. It was great!"

"What did everybody say? Did they laugh or what?"

"No," Lymie said, all excited again. "That's what's so amazing! Those heads musta been so ugly they looked real. Everybody was going crazy. You'd think they'd found gold or something. When they took the heads away, they gave 'em a police escort!"

"Wow." I sat down. "Wow." I thought for a second. "Lymie, I'm not sure this is so good . . ."

Other Avon Flare Books by
Daniel Hayes
Coming Soon

NO EFFECT

EYE
OF THE
BEHOLDER

DANIEL HAYES

Best wishes,
Daniel Hayes
Delmar, NY

AN AVON FLARE BOOK

AVON BOOKS
A division of
The Hearst Corporation
1350 Avenue of the Americas
New York, New York 10019

Copyright © 1992 by Daniel Hayes
Published by arrangement with David R. Godine, Publisher, Inc.
Library of Congress Catalog Card Number: 92-29565
ISBN: 0-380-72285-2
RL: 5.6

First Avon Flare Printing: June 1994

AVON FLARE TRADEMARK REG. U.S. PAT. OFF. AND IN OTHER COUNTRIES, MARCA REGISTRADA, HECHO EN U.S.A.

Printed in the U.S.A.

RA   10 9 8 7 6 5 4 3 2

1

Almost four days to the hour after Lymie got there, I clocked him on the head with a book so humongous I almost wrenched my back throwing it. It was the blue medical book Mom had left on my nightstand, opened to the chicken pox page. Mom was pretty mad, so I didn't even try telling her it was kind of her fault for supplying me with ammunition when she knew Lymie and I were fighting. Besides, she'd've just told me that nobody normal would ever even *think* of using a book as ammunition and that as soon as I got better we were going to have a serious discussion about things. And then she'd probably remind me that it was my idea to have Lymie stay with me in the first place.

Which it was. After three days of being sick alone, I was going crazy. I had a headache and chills and I was driving Mom up the wall with my whining (so she said), although I thought I'd been pretty good considering how lousy I felt and how I'd been cooped up all that time in a room by myself like some kind of prisoner. So when Lymie called to tell me he had the chicken pox too, the first thing I thought of (when I got done laughing) was that he should come over to my house and we could be sick together. Our mothers finally decided it was a good idea too. Then they could take turns watching us instead of them both being stuck with one of us full time.

Things were pretty decent at first. Mom had Chuckie, our groundskeeper, move the bed out of my brother Christopher's room and put it up in my room. Then Lymie's mother drove Lymie over and we were in business. As soon as everybody cleared out, Lymie dug this crumpled up piece of paper out of his pocket.

"Hey, Ty, listen to this," he told me. "It's from the nurse. It's about you." He started reading. Lymie speed.

DEAR PARENTS:

THIS IS TO ALERT YOU TO THE FACT THAT YOUR CHILD HAD BEEN EXPOSED TO CHICKEN POX. IF YOUR CHILD HAS NOT YET HAD CHICKEN POX, HE IS . . . VUL . . . VUL SOMETHING . . .

I went over and sat next to him. "Vulnerable," I said, looking at the word he was pointing at. He continued.

VULNERABLE. INITIAL SYMPTOMS INCLUDE A LOW-GRADE FEVER, MALE . . . OR MAYBE MAL . . .

I grabbed the note. "It's malaise," I told him and then kept reading it myself.

INITIAL SYMPTOMS INCLUDE A LOW-GRADE FEVER, MALAISE, AND WITHIN TWENTY-FOUR HOURS THE APPEARANCE OF A RASH. INFECTED CHILDREN MUST BE KEPT HOME FOR AT LEAST A WEEK BUT MAY RETURN TO SCHOOL AS SOON AS ALL LESIONS ARE CRUSTED; THE CRUSTS ARE NOT INFECTIOUS.

"Gross," I said. "I'm not going back to school if I'm still all crusted."

2

"Me either," Lymie said. "We'll have to keep acting sick until we look normal again."

"You might never get to go back," I told him.

Lymie clubbed me with his pillow. "You never woulda even started school if you hadda wait to look normal." He paused for a second and thought. "What about malaise? You think we got that yet?" He lay back on his bed and looked up studying me.

I already knew "malaise" from seeing it in the medical book. I tried to look all serious. "It usually means you turn green and start barfing all over the place. People used to foam at the mouth when they had it, but that's kinda rare now with modern medications."

Lymie sat up and gawked at me harder than ever. "You're kidding me, right?"

I kind of toyed with the idea of shrugging my shoulders and handing him the medical book so he could check it out himself, which he never would've done in a million years, but I didn't. Lymie's got this chubby, intense-looking face that gets all scrunched up when he's worried, and it's hard to put him on without feeling like some kind of lowlife.

"Nah," I told him. "It just means feeling sick. You know, cruddy . . . lousy. Like we've already *been* feeling."

"Thank God." He clubbed me another one with his pillow and then slumped back on his bed and took a deep breath. He looked so relieved I was glad I hadn't lied.

The next few days chugged along pretty much like that. A lot of busting on each other and plenty of pillow attacks, but nothing major. Lymie and I watched about twenty movies on my VCR and played video games until we thought our wrists would fall off. Some of the time we spent telling each other how great our lives were going to be. I was going to be an actor like my brother Christopher and my mom, and I was going to work out with weights and do calisthenics till I was tough like Chuckie. Lymie would never admit that he wasn't tough already, so he didn't say anything about working out. He thought he might want to be a director, but he wasn't too sure. He was still going through that stage where he was thinking about maybe being a cop. Only he didn't want to work for a police department or anything. He just wanted to do it on his own. Kind of like Superman or Spiderman but without the costume. I told him he could go by the name Spazman because that one wasn't taken, and I cracked up. He did too. After he clubbed me again with his pillow, that is.

After forty-eight hours of this kind of thing though, the honeymoon was over. All the dumb things Lymie had a habit of saying—like his idea about being a supersleuth—were starting to grate on my nerves. And Lymie wasn't exactly thrilled about me constantly pointing out to him just how dumb his ideas were. Not only that, but I require about twice as much sleep as Lymie, and it seemed like every time I dozed off, he'd whack me over the head with a pillow and ask me what I wanted to do. It never dawned on him that what I wanted to do was sleep. We were quite a team. Lymie was mad when I was sleeping, and I was mad when I wasn't.

How I ended up clocking Lymie with the medical book was he woke me up for about the tenth time that day and I lay there smoldering, not looking at him or answering him or anything. Then he got feeling sorry for himself and he said it. The same thing he'd been saying for days, and each time it made me a little crazier.

"If it wasn't for you, I wouldn't even have the chicken pox."

"Lymie, you're such a lamebrain!" I yelled, yanking up off the bed like I was on a string or something. "How many times have I gotta tell you? You didn't get the stupid chicken pox from me!"

He didn't answer because he knew what I was going to say next.

"Listen," I told him. "You got the chicken pox the day after I did, right?"

Silence.

"Yes or no. You either did or you didn't, right? So say it—yes or no."

4

He sat there wearing that pudgy blank look he gets whenever he wants to shield himself from information.

"Yes," I answered for him. "You got the chicken pox one day after I did. You can ask my mother. Ask your mother. Ask anybody!"

Lymie rolled his eyes. He knew the routine.

"And according to this book . . ." I picked up the medical book. "According to this book, chicken pox takes at least ten days to develop after you've been exposed to it. That's incubation period, goofis, and it's a scientific fact!"

Lymie leaned back on his headboard and took this smug-sounding deep breath. "So?"

"SO YOU DIDN'T GET THEM FROM ME!" I poked my head out toward him. "IT GOES AGAINST SCIENCE! WE BOTH GOT THEM FROM SOME INFECTED KID ABOUT TEN DAYS BEFORE WE EVEN KNEW IT!" I started waving the book around in the air as a kind of warning even though I knew that wouldn't stop him.

"Then how come you got them first?" he said. "And how come the nurse sends home a notice warning us about you spreading diseases around the school?"

Unfortunately for Lymie, the book had been in the middle of a major wave in his direction when he finished, and all I had to do was crank on a little more steam and let it ride. He had just enough time to flinch back a few inches or it would've caught him right between the eyes. As it was, the book skipped off the side of his head and took the lamp off his nightstand.

By the time my mother got there, Lymie was bouncing up and down on top of me with his fingers twisted around my neck. He was so wrapped up in what he was doing he didn't even hear Mom yelling. Of course it didn't help that she was yelling *my* name, which she always does whenever we fight, same as Lymie's mother always yells *his* name, no matter who's getting strangled or belted at the time.

When Lymie finally realized Mom was in the room and he let go of me, the first thing he did was to start rubbing the side of his head. Then he went over and picked up the lamp and set it on his nightstand and put the medical book back on mine. Like some kind of tattling mime. That really ticked me off. I mean, if you're going to rat on somebody, you should at least do it in words.

"Timothy Tyler McAllister," Mom said, planting her hands on her hips and putting on this flabbergasted face, "did you throw that book at Lymie?"

"He was bothering me." I started rubbing my neck where Lymie'd strangled me, hoping maybe I could land a little sympathy too.

Mom sat on my bed and looked at me for a second. Then she picked up the medical book, not like she was going to read it, but more like you'd heft a rock or something. Her other hand came up under my jaw and wrapped its fingers around my cheeks. Next thing I knew, the book was in my face.

"*Look* at this thing," she said. "Are you trying to kill somebody?"

I looked at it. It *was* pretty huge. "I was just trying to make him shut up."

I heard this big sigh come out of her. "You know what I think about hitting people."

"You don't believe in it," I said and tried not to sound bored.

"And why don't I believe in it?"

When I hesitated for a second, I could feel her fingers tighten on my jaw and the book started waving a little. "You don't think it solves anything," I told her.

"And . . . ?"

"And you think it's wrong and barbaric," I said, rolling my eyes.

The fingers dug in a little. "Let's not push our luck," she said. Her other hand was waving the book harder now, like her throwing arm might be getting itchy. "Believe me, if I thought it'd do any good . . ." The book was bobbing around right in front of my nose. "But in this house we don't hit—for *any* reason." The book went down and she

6

cranked my head around until we were eye to eye. "Do we understand each other?"

I kind of wanted to ask her about her views on strangling, for Lymie's benefit, but her fingers were still locked around my cheeks and I could feel they wanted me to nod, so I did.

When Mom left, she took the medical book with her.

That evening, Lymie's father started coming over after he finished his farm work. Which was probably no big coincidence since I'd also noticed that Mom had Chuckie start painting the hallway right outside my room. Chuckie *had* been finishing up as much of the outside work as he could before the cold weather arrived, and the weather was still great, so that wasn't it. I figured that moving him inside during the day, and bringing in Mr. Lawrence at night, was part of some kind of riot control plan.

"Why don't you just send for Mrs. Saunders?" I said to Mom when I realized what was going on. "Next thing you know, you'll be dragging people in off the street." Mrs. Saunders was our housekeeper and she'd been visiting her sister in Burbank since a few days before I got sick. She's one of the few people I know who doesn't believe you can spoil a kid with kindness. Especially a sick kid. I'd already thought about calling her a few times and letting it slip how I was sick and miserable because I knew she'd come running.

Mom shook her head. "Do you really think it's necessary to ruin the only vacation Mrs. Saunders has taken in over a year because we have two boys here who are too immature to share a room like civilized young men?"

That's the kind of question you can't possibly say yes to without looking like an idiot. Besides, feeling guilty over maybe ruining Mrs. Saunders's vacation was why I hadn't called her myself.

"I was just thinking about *you*," I said, kind of smirking to myself at how I'd gotten out of having to say no.

"That's very kind of you, dear, but we'll manage to

struggle through this on our own." And then she gave this sigh like maybe she wasn't too sure.

I didn't really see what the big deal was. Sure, Lymie and I fought some, but we weren't all *that* bad. And our mothers weren't all that defenseless either. Lymie's mother alone probably could have put an end to World War II if she'd been there and it'd been bothering her. And if that didn't work, my mother could have *reasoned* with the armies, telling them how on *this* planet we don't fight, until they all decided it'd be easier just to forget the whole thing.

Lymie's father didn't seem too bent out of shape by having to be there. He'd sit on a chair between our beds reading his newspaper. Out loud. And looking for audience participation.

"Says here," he told us one night in this hokey twang I was pretty sure he put on for my benefit because I'd never lived in the country before, "says here that two fellas robbed a convenience store in New York City and when they went to make their getaway, their car had been stolen." He chuckled. "Now how about that?"

"City people," Lymie sneered, leaning up so he could look right at me.

"Shut up," I told him.

Mr. Lawrence kept chuckling to himself just like nobody'd even said anything. A few minutes later he came out with, "Hmm, now here's something interestin'. Looks like we're in for some big doings around here."

"Yeah?" Lymie said. "Like what?"

"Well," he said after he took his time and skimmed the article a little more, "Remember that famous Eye-talian artist by the name of Badoglio that spent a few years in Wakefield as a young man?"

"Badoglio?" I said, sitting up. "Yeah, I heard of him. He used to do sculptures and stuff."

"Some artist," Lymie said. "He made ugly rock heads with big noses."

Mr. Lawrence laughed. "What we consider ugly rock heads with big noses are considered valuable treasures by them that know art and understand it. I s'pose they see things in it the rest of us miss."

"So what about the . . . the big doings?" I was hoping I wouldn't still be all crusted over if something big was about to happen.

"Well, let me see," Mr. Lawrence said. He rocked back in his chair and studied the paper some more. "Says here they're planning some kind of festival in Academy Park to celebrate the centennial of Badoglio's birth. They've got a traveling Badoglio exhibit coming in. There's a whole schedule of events here. There'll be art critics, a crafts show, activities for the kids, food booths . . ."

"Food booths?" Lymie said, perking right up.

"Your stomach is really artistic, Lyme," I said.

"Shut up," he told me and leaned over behind his father and tried to belt me. I scooted to the far side of my bed.

"Hey, boys, I'd forgotten about this part," Mr. Lawrence continued. Listen to this:

LEGEND HAS IT THAT IN 1912, IN A FIT OF DEPRESSION, THE HIGHLY EMOTIONAL YOUNG BADOGLIO RUSHED OUT OF HIS HOUSE IN THE MIDDLE OF THE NIGHT AND THREW TWO OF HIS PARTIALLY COMPLETED HEADS INTO THE HOOSICKILL RIVER. NEXT SATURDAY, A WEEK BEFORE THE CELEBRATION, THE SECTION OF THE HOOSICKILL IN THE VICINITY OF BADOGLIO'S FORMER HOUSE WILL BE DREDGED IN THE HOPE OF FINDING ONE OF THESE LOST TREASURES.

He closed the paper and looked up beaming. "That'd be something, huh, boys? Wouldn't that put Wakefield on the map if they were to find something?"

"Are they gonna have food booths at the dredging?" Lymie wanted to know.

Mom came in and made us turn out the lights at ten o'clock. For once I wasn't tired.

"That's pretty neat, Lymie. You know, about that

9

Badoglio guy. You think he really did chuck those heads in the river?"

"Probably," Lymie said. "Who'd make up a story like that?"

"But why? After all the work he must've done on them?"

" 'Cause he knew they stunk," Lymie said.

"Come on, Lyme. They couldn't've stunk too bad if they're considered valuable treasures now."

"Tyler, did you ever see that guy's work?"

"No."

"Then don't tell me they don't stink. We used to have to look at pictures of that guy's stuff in art class and I'm serious, he couldn't chisel his way out of a paper bag."

"Maybe you just don't understand art, like your father says."

"Maybe not. But I understand ugly, and any rock that guy ever touched turned out ugly, believe me."

"I'd still like to see some of his stuff." I'm always curious about things like that. I even watch public TV sometimes when Lymie isn't around.

"You sure you want to see it?" Lymie said. "Knowing you, it'll probably give you nightmares."

"Funny, Lyme," I told him, "but I'll worry about my own nightmares."

"Yeah, well don't say I didn't warn you. I'm telling you, Ty, the two of us could make better heads than that guy did."

If I had an alarm in my head that'd go off every time I heard something that could lead to serious trouble, it would've been ringing like crazy right then.

But I didn't hear a thing.

The next day I had Mom go through Dad's library downstairs to find out if there were any books on Badoglio. I figured there would be. My father had been a real booklover and his collection was huge. I remember how when I was a little kid he was always strict about not wanting me to fiddle around in his office or mess things up around the rest of the house, but he always made me feel welcome in his library. He'd even built up quite a collection of kids' books for my brother Christopher when he was little and he kept adding to it when I was that age. Mom used to joke that the library was one of the reasons she had to buy such a big house when we moved to Wakefield.

Mom came up ten minutes later with a book. It wasn't just about Badoglio but it was on all kinds of modern art and Mom told us Badoglio'd be in it. She handed the book to Lymie.

"I'll leave this with you, Lyman," she said, "because I know *you* won't throw it." She kind of cocked her eyebrow at me and then left.

Lymie gave me this little smirk and then sat up on the

edge of his bed and started thumbing through the book. "Wait'll you see this guy's work, Ty. You won't believe it." He thumbed through some more pages. "How're ya supposed to find anything in here anyway? This book is huge."

"Use the index," I told him and sat up on the edge of my bed. "In the back. Just look up under Badoglio."

He flipped to the back, found the B's, and started sliding his finger up and down the columns. All of a sudden his eyes got big. "Whoa, hold the phone, Alice. *This* I gotta check out."

"What?"

"It says on page 162 there's something called *The Bride Stripped Bare by Her Bachelors.*"

"Yeah?" I said and went over and sat next to him.

Lymie's fingers were flipping pages so fast he was risking a serious paper cut, and at the same time he was deliberately holding the book so I couldn't see anything. Finally he stopped flipping and gawked at one of the pages. "I must've read the wrong page. There's no bride here." He went back to the index again. "I don't get it, Ty. It says 162."

"Lemme see it." I grabbed the book and went to 162. When I got there, I started skimming through the pictures. "It *is* the right page, Lyme," I said, pointing at the caption under one of the pictures. "Look, *The Bride Stripped Bare by Her Bachelors, Even.* I wonder what the *Even* part means."

Lymie didn't care about the *Even* part. He grabbed the book back and scowled down at the page. "What a rip-off! There's not even any people there."

I leaned in and studied the picture. "There might be," I told him. "See those things off to the side that look kinda like clothespins? I think they're supposed to be people. And see that big window in front? It's probably supposed to be like we're peeping in through that window at them."

Lymie snorted. "Big thrill. Who wants to spy on a bunch of clothespins?" He scrunched up his face and studied the picture some more. He even flipped the page over like he was trying to see if there was an answer on the back or something. All of a sudden he started cracking up. "That's pretty funny. Did you do this, Ty?"

I looked down and saw that he was pointing at this picture of the *Mona Lisa*. I shrugged. "Whaddaya mean?"

"Look closer," Lymie said, all excited. "She's gotta mustache."

I leaned in closer. She did. And not only that but somebody'd stuck a little goatee on her too.

"I didn't do that," I said.

"Your brother?"

"I doubt it."

Lymie looked at me. "Your *father*?" He almost whispered it. My father had been killed when the private jet he'd been in had gone down in the mountains of northern Arizona, before we'd moved to Wakefield. Lymie never mentioned him. His mother or somebody probably told him not to.

I shook my head. "No way." I grabbed the book and studied it some more. "Look," I said. "You have to read the captions. This is the way it's *supposed* to be. It says some artist named Duchamp took a print of the *Mona Lisa* and did that with a pencil."

"An *artist* did that?" Lymie looked like he couldn't believe it.

"Yeah," I told him, "and he gave it a name, *L. H. O. O. Q.*, which probably stands for something. It's owned by Mrs. Mary Sherman in New York." I gave the book back to him.

"He got paid *money* to do that?"

I nodded. "Yeah, and how much you wanna bet that Mrs. Mary Sherman has like a Park Avenue address and paid about a million dollars for that thing?"

This whistling sound came out of Lymie. "I coulda done that," he said. "I think I *have* done that."

I laughed. "You probably have, knowing you."

Lymie flipped through a few more pages and then his

head bobbed in for a closer look. "Yeeow! Now tell me that's not disgusting."

I looked where he was pointing. There were these two really chunky ladies, completely naked and facing each other. They looked like they were doing some kind of X-rated show and tell.

"That *is* disgusting, Lyme. Sincerely." I read the caption. This one was called *Two Nudes* and it was by Picasso. I poked Lymie. "It oughta be called *Two Fat Nudes with Faces That Could Stop a Clock*."

Lymie was too amazed to even laugh. "If you were gonna paint naked women, why would you choose fat ones? What a waste of paint."

We heard this kind of pretend-to-clear-your-voice "ah-hem" from the doorway. It was Mom. First she was standing there, and then she was walking toward us. Mom knew a thing or two about art, and I figured she was planning on broadening our horizons.

"Many of Picasso's women were full-figured," she told us. "You know, this notion that women must be thin to be attractive is a pretty recent phenomenon. In many cultures and throughout much of history a woman with a little substance to her was often considered quite beautiful. And thinness was considered a sign of poor health." She stood in front of us with her hands on her hips.

"A little substance?" I said. "Those ladies have more rolls than a bakery. Didn't they ever hear of Lean Cuisine back then?"

"The point I'm trying to make . . ." Mom stopped and drew in a deep breath. "The point is . . . different people define beauty differently. I do hope as you get older, Tyler, you'll become more open-minded and tolerant."

"I think what you're saying is great," Lymie piped up.

I glared over at him.

"Thank you, Lyman," Mom said and gave him a big smile.

"Yeah," Lymie continued, "it's good to know that even if you're born ugly or something, there might be a place you can go where people'll think you look decent."

I roared and clapped Lymie on the back. "He got you, Mom!"

Lymie started laughing too, but not right away. Sometimes I think he doesn't even say the stuff he says to be funny.

Mom groaned and shook her head. "Well," she said, "I can see that the two of you deserve each other." She looked at us. "Didn't you tell me you wanted that book so you could learn about Benito Badoglio?"

"We did," I said. "Only Lymie decided to check out some nudes first."

"I did not," Lymie said, giving me an elbow. Then to Mom, "I found those fat ladies by accident."

Mom smiled. "Let me see if I can help you. We wouldn't want any more accidents now, would we?" She took the book and found where the Badoglio stuff was. "Ah, here's what we want." She set the book back on Lymie's lap.

Lymie and I gawked down at it. First there was a smeary-looking painting of a guy playing a violin. Then there were two samples of Badoglio's sculptures. They were just heads with no bodies and they sat on these square pedestals. The backs of their heads were squared off too, as if he hadn't gotten around to finishing them. And both heads had these long, horse faces and huge noses like they'd been bred to sniff out drugs or something.

"What'd I tell ya, Ty?" Lymie said. "Ugly or what?"

I nodded. "There's no 'or what' about it," I told him.

"All right, all right," Mom said and sat down on the other side of Lymie. "I can see you two need a little lesson in art." She pointed at Badoglio's first head. "You see, boys, the narrow eyes and the straight elongated nose . . . these were characteristic of all of Badoglio's portraits. It represents classical beauty."

"Give me a break, Mom. A good plastic surgeon could have made a fortune just by fixing the people on this one page." I poked Lymie and we both cracked up.

I heard this big sigh come out of Mom. Then she stood

up. "Fine," she said. "If you want to grow up to be narrow-minded about the fine arts . . ."

"Fine arts, Mom?" I told her. "One guy in this book penciled in a mustache and a goatee on the *Mona Lisa.* You call that fine arts?"

Mom smiled. "Oh, you mean the piece by Duchamp?" Only she said it more like *Dooshaw.* "I grant you it's debatable whether that piece qualifies as fine art. He may have meant it simply as a joke, but many critics have seen Duchamp's treatment of the *Mona Lisa* as a symbol of his view of life's meaninglessness."

You had to give her credit trying to explain all this to the two of us.

"So what do the letters stand for?" Lymie wanted to know.

"Well, that's part of the joke," Mom said, kind of surprised that one of us cared. "*L. H. O. O. Q.* is phonetic for the French *elle a chaud au cul.*"

"Meaning . . . ?" I said.

I'm pretty sure she started to blush, and that hardly ever happens to Mom. "Well, as politely as I can put it, it means something like *she has a hot rear end.*"

Lymie and I were dying. We laughed so hard we both collapsed back across his bed. And we couldn't've stopped laughing if Mom had put a gun to our heads. Every once in a while one of us would catch our breath enough to spit out, "The *Mona Lisa's* got a hot butt!" and then we'd punch each other and crack up all over again. And all that time Mom was just standing there with her arms folded, wearing this half smile and looking down at us like we'd just escaped from some place with padded rooms.

Finally she'd had enough. "You're both beyond hope," she said and started for the door. "But listen up," she told us before she left. "You can laugh at Picasso all you want, and you can laugh at Duchamp, but I'd be a little careful about making jokes about Badoglio around here. The people of Wakefield are very proud of him, and a lot of them won't think some of your comments are so funny." She gave us the evil eye, but it didn't do any good. We were still cracking up.

After Mom left and we both caught our breath enough to sit up, Lymie grabbed the modern art book and looked up under "nude" to see if he could find any good ones. He checked out *Nude Descending a Staircase, Nudes in the Forest, Nude with a Mirror*, and *Nude Woman with a Basket of Fruit*, before he got disgusted and slammed the book shut. "I give up, Ty. You wanna give it a shot?"

"Nah," I said and grabbed the remote and flicked on the TV. Except for checking out the big Badoglio celebration, I didn't really want to have anything more to do with modern art.

3

On Thursday the doctor said we could go back to school the next day. Lymie and I were both still blotched up enough so that we didn't want to be caught dead in school. We tried acting sick some more, but nobody bought it. Then we begged and whined until Mom finally gave in. Only because the next day was Friday. Mrs. Lawrence said Lymie could stay home too, but both of them said we were going to school Monday no matter how stupid we thought we looked.

Mom was supposed to meet Mrs. Oster at the country club that Friday morning for golf and lunch, but Mrs. Oster called at the last minute and cancelled. Another poodle problem. She cancelled every time her dog sniffled.

"I don't know why you put up with her, Mom," I said. "She's not dependable. She's always having conniptions about that dumb mutt."

"She worries about Reginald," Mom said. "She can't help it."

"Reginald," I sneered. "Who ever heard of a dog named Reginald? What's his problem this time? He got a flea or something and she's gotta call in a SWAT team?" I poked Lymie and we both laughed.

"Very funny," Mom said, "but if you recall, I cancelled last week because *you* were sick."

"Well, I'm not some dumb mutt."

"No, but you are my little teddy bear!" She came over and started squeezing my cheeks and saying, "Aren't you? You're still my little teddy bear, aren't you?" She used to always do that teddy bear routine when I was little. Now she only did it whenever she wanted to shut me up.

"Come on, Mom. Cut it out!" I tried to duck my head under the covers.

I heard her laugh on the way out. No sooner was she gone than I could feel Lymie's eyes on me, so I picked up the modern art book and cranked it behind my head, all ready to let it fly.

"Don't even say it," I said.

An hour passed. I was bored. Every once in a while Lymie'd call me Teddy and try to pinch my cheeks and I'd wing something at him, but nothing big and without much enthusiasm. Finally I climbed out of bed and got dressed.

"Hey, Lymie. Come 'ere."

Lymie dragged himself out of bed and came over by me.

"Look out that window, Lyme."

"At what?"

"What do you mean, at what? Look outside. Look around. It's like the nicest day of the whole fall. It looks like something out of a New England postcard."

"So?"

I looked at him and shook my head. "So . . . so on a day like this we shouldn't be cooped up here like a couple of convicts."

"Hey, it's either this or school." He padded back to his bed.

"There's gotta be a third choice," I said. "Like I've been thinking about those heads Badoglio was supposed to have

19

chucked into the Hoosickill River. I was thinking . . ."

"I thought you thought they were stupid-looking."

"I do. But I was thinking, what if *we* were to find those things? Before anybody else. We'd probably be heroes or something."

"Forget it, Ty. For one thing, your mother's not going to let us out of the house. For another thing, Badoglio's house was way over by the country club and my bike is home. I wouldn't walk all that way even if we could."

The door opened and Mom came in. "Mrs. Oster is back from the vet and Reginald is fine. She wants me to meet her for lunch at the club, but I've already sent Chuckie to Saratoga for a few things, and I hate to leave you two alone."

I looked at Lymie and smiled. If I played my cards right, by noontime we'd be out in the sunshine scoping out the area around Badoglio's house.

"One hour," Mom said as we got out of the car. "I'll be out in one hour. And stay in the sun. You can't be too careful after you've been sick."

She felt my head and Lymie's head one last time and looked at us like we were two delicate China dolls or something.

"Hey, Mom, don't sweat it. Go in and have lunch. This fresh air'll do us good. We'll be here on the putting green. In the sun." I turned toward the green so my face wouldn't give me away.

"Boys? Didn't you forget something?"

I looked at Lymie. He looked at me.

"Your putters!" Mom said. She laughed and opened the trunk.

"Oh, yeah." I gave a little laugh. "It must be those chicken pox made us absent-minded."

"She's gone," I said. "Let's go."

We leaned our putters against a tree and took off for the third fairway.

"I gotta give you credit," Lymie said. "I never thought you'd pull it off. I was sure your mother'd say no."

"She did say no," I said, "but the mighty Tyler has the power to turn a no into a yes." Only I didn't tell him how I did it. It was too embarrassing. First I went down and sat next to her in the living room. Then I sighed a few times and kind of leaned back against her. And whenever I felt her looking at me, I gave her these sad eyes to try to melt her down. I had her eating out of my hand in five minutes. The scary thing is that Reginald probably does the same kind of thing to get around Mrs. Oster. And *he* makes me sick.

When we crossed the third fairway, these three guys started yelling at us. If Mom or somebody had been with us, they would have smiled and waved us by, but it kills people at a country club to see kids roaming around on their own. They probably figure if they're rich enough to join a country club, they shouldn't have to put up with kids. We ran to the side and ducked down over the embankment that leads to the river. Half climbing and half sliding on our butts, we made it to the bottom. Lymie pointed left and we trudged along the riverbank.

Before I knew it, Lymie grabbed my arm. Hidden among the trees and brush was an old cobblestone foundation. You could barely see it. I plowed my way through the brush and peered into the open cellar. A big pile of stones lay on one side, probably from the old chimney. The rest of the floor was littered with empty beer cans and old cigarette packages. I climbed down on the stones and started scrounging around. Lymie sat on the foundation watching me.

"What happened to the rest of the house, Lymie?"

"It burnt down way back when my father was a kid."

I looked around and tried to picture what it might have been like in Badoglio's day. Then I spotted something sticking out of the ground and grabbed it. "Hey, Lymie, look. An old spoon. It might have been Badoglio's. You think it's worth anything?"

"Yeah, right, Tyler," Lymie sneered. "I bet if we could find a rusty fork and a butter knife, we'd be set for life."

"You've got a lousy attitude, Lyme. Plus you're stupid. If any of this stuff was Badoglio's, it makes it memorabilia. You know—historical. And historical stuff is worth a bundle."

"Look, Ty! Over there! A bunch of Badoglio's old Budweiser cans! We struck it rich!" He slapped his knee and started yucking it up for all he was worth.

I groaned. "Give it up, Lyme. If it wasn't for your face, you wouldn't be funny at all." I dropped the old spoon and climbed out of the cellar, figuring if there had been any memorabilia there, somebody probably grabbed it years ago. I studied the bushes in front of the foundation to see if I could make out any old path to the river that Badoglio might've used. I couldn't, so I plowed back out through my own path.

I stopped when I got to the riverbank. "This would probably be about where Badoglio chucked those heads in," I said.

"*If* he chucked the heads in," Lymie added, coming up behind me.

We both stood there for a minute staring into the water. I was hoping to spot one of those heads staring back at us.

"We're not going to find anything from here," I said finally, and started taking off my sneakers and socks and rolling up my pant legs as far as I could. "Maybe if we kinda wade around, we'll get lucky."

"Hey, Tyler, look! I think I see one of those ugly heads!"

"Where?" I said, getting all excited.

"Oh, sorry. My mistake. It was your reflection."

That cracked him up. It doesn't take much.

"You can stand around looking stupid if you want, Lyme, but I'm gonna see what I can find."

"Be careful of broken glass and stuff, Tyler. If you get the water all bloody, we won't be able to see anything."

I looked at him. I couldn't tell if he was joking or not. Probably not, knowing him. One thing I did know. He wanted to get his hands on those heads as much as I did. He was already taking off his sneakers.

"We'll start downstream," I said. "Then we won't rile up the water where we're looking."

We moved about twenty yards downstream and stood there on the edge staring into the water.

"You don't think there's snapping turtles or anything in there, do you, Lymie?" I once saw a snapping turtle chomp off the end of a stick that was almost as thick as my wrist. I didn't want one of them chomping on my toes.

"Nah," Lymie said. Only he didn't sound too sure. And he didn't get in the water.

I found a stick and poked it around the bottom. Nothing grabbed it. The bottom was all squishy and gooey. Not the kind of place where you'd want to stick your feet. I waited a minute for the water to clear. I gawked at Lymie. He gawked back.

"Well, here goes nothing." I lowered a foot into the water. As I set my weight on it, it disappeared into the goo. "Aaaaah!" I yelled. I tried to pull it back but it was stuck there like a suction cup. I had no choice but to stick my other foot in. "Yick," I said as it disappeared along with my first foot. "This stuff's gross."

"Relax, Ty. It's only mud."

"Then what are you doing out there?"

"I'm coming. I'm coming. Don't get hyper." Lymie stuck his big toe gingerly through the water into the goo and pulled it back.

"It's only mud," I said.

"Yeah, but lotsa nasty things *live* in mud."

"How come you didn't remember that when *I* was getting in?" I glared at him until he plopped his foot down behind mine. He grabbed my shoulder as his foot sank.

"Gross!" he yelled as his second foot disappeared.

"Hands off, Lymie! You're gonna make me fall."

"No," Lymie said. "I'm gonna stop me from falling."

He finally let go and we both started working our way upstream, our arms outstretched like we were doing a highwire act or something. We moved slow, giving the turtles or whatever plenty of time to get out of our way. Still, before long we were all the way up past Badoglio's house.

"We've got to head out for deeper water," I said. "If this Badoglio guy was having some kind of a fit like the legend says, he wouldn't have just plunked the heads down on the side. He'd've really wung 'em out there."

I headed for deeper water and Lymie followed.

"My pants are getting soaked," he grumbled.

"So shut up and roll your cuffs up furth . . ."

My foot dropped off some kind of a ledge and it didn't land until the water was up around my waist.

"Ooooooh!" I gasped. "That's cold!"

"Good move, Ty."

"Whew!" I stood there trying to catch my breath. "As long as I'm wet . . . I might as well . . . see if I can . . . find anything."

I started sliding my feet around the bottom trying to feel what was down there. The ground was firmer now and easier to manage but my feet were so cold they actually hurt, and my legs weren't feeling much better. I couldn't stay in much longer.

"Lymie, I feel something. It feels like a big rock."

"No kidding, Ty? Can you feel a face on it?"

"Feels too smooth."

"That might be the back of its head. Flip it over."

I pried it with my foot till I almost fell in. "It won't budge. I gotta get my hands on it."

I bent over and stuck my arm down as far as I could without getting the rest of me totally soaked. "I can't reach it."

I stretched further and felt the icy water reaching around my shoulder and seeping through the left side of my shirt. Dipping my face in the water and opening my eyes, I saw the rock and grabbed it. Working my hand and foot together, I finally broke it free.

"I've got it!" I yelled. "I've got it!"

"Great!" Lymie said. "What is it?"

I lifted it out of the water. I turned it around in my hands. I stared down at it.

"It's a rock! A stupid rock! I'm practically scuba diving and all I end up with is a lousy *rock*!"

"Well, that's only the first one," Lymie said. "Keep looking."

"*You* keep looking," I said. "I'm freezing my butt. I can't even feel my feet anymore!"

I dropped the rock.

I was wrong. I *could* feel my feet.

I sat on the shore shivering like crazy. And my teeth were chattering like jackhammers. The only part of me that was dry was my right shoulder and part of my back.

"That's chilly water," Lymie said.

"Tell me about it." I clenched my jaw to stop the chattering. "Let's get to the car before I freeze to death."

"Wow, look at you, Ty. You're a mess. You oughta at least rinse your feet off."

I stuck my feet back in the water and squished them around till they were white again. Then I examined them for bloodsuckers. Then I stood up and tried to brush off my rear end. Only the water from my pants had turned the dirt under me to mud, and you just don't brush off mud.

"Come on," I said. "Grab your sneaks. Maybe this crud'll start to dry by the time we get back."

Lymie and I scaled up the bank, being careful not to cut our feet on rocks and branches. As soon as we hit the fairway, I started running. I felt like my whole body was turning blue. Plus, I figured the extra breeze might help dry me out some. Lymie lumbered along after me.

A couple of guys on the putting green gave me a funny look as I went by, but I didn't care. I had bigger problems on my mind. Like whether I should go in the clubhouse to get Mom or freeze to death. When I looked down at myself, I decided on the freezing. I headed for the car. Luckily it was in the sun.

Reginald was tied to the chain link fence in front of Mom's car. When he spotted us, he started yapping like crazy.

"Quick," I said. "Get in the car before Mrs. Oster comes out to see what Reginald's problem is." I opened the door and felt this great blast of heat.

"Hey, stupid!" Lymie grabbed my arm. "You gonna get in the car like that?"

I reached back and felt the mud I was wearing.

"Aw, crap!" I slammed the door and thought for a minute. Then I tossed my sneakers and socks up on the hood and climbed up after them, stretching myself across it face down so I wouldn't smear it with mud. The hood was pretty hot from the sun and it felt good. I could hear Reginald yapping and jumping up against the car.

"Lymie, you gotta shut that dumb mutt up until I get dry. Play with him or something."

I cranked my head around so I could see Reginald. What a dopey-looking dog! He was a white poodle with one of those stupid haircuts where they left a puff of hair on the top of his head and around his knees and ankles, and they left his chest the way it was so he looked like he was wearing a wool sweater. The kind of haircut you'd give a dog if your main purpose was to humiliate him. But Reginald wasn't very normal anyway. He was so hyper he couldn't sit still and shut up for two seconds. He always had to be running around yipping like he'd just stuck his tongue in an electric socket or something.

Lymie reached down and tried to pet him but that just made him more spastic. He started jumping around in circles trying to nip Lymie's hands. Finally Lymie got frustrated and snatched him up in his arms and plopped him down on the hood with me with his legs still going ninety miles an hour. Reginald took off across the hood and skidded to a halt up by my head. Before I knew it he started licking my ears and my face.

"Arrrgh!" I yelled. "Lymie, get him away!" I can never understand why anybody'd let a dog lick their face. Your face always ends up smelling like dog breath.

Lymie laughed. "At least he's quiet now."

I turned the other way and hid my face under my arms. Reginald poked around trying to find my face for a minute and then he stopped, probably thinking about what he should do next. Pretty soon he climbed up on my back, growled a little, and started yanking on my shirt. I could feel him give my rear end a few head butts.

"That dog's sick," Lymie said.

"I coulda told you that," I said.

"Hey, Tyler, you gotta check this out. Look at his face!"

I twisted around and peered out from under my arms. "Oh, no!"

Reginald's face looked like it had been dipped in mud. Which it had, kind of.

"Lymie, you jerk! You know what Mrs. Oster's gonna say when she sees him? She's gonna have a bird!"

"Hey, it's not my butt he got the mud off of."

"Who cares whose butt it was? You stood there like an idiot and watched him do it."

"Well, you *laid* there like an idiot and *let* him do it."

I jumped down to the ground. Reginald raced around in circles, leaving a trail of dirty footprints across the hood and barking loud enough to wake the dead. I grabbed for him and missed. He snatched up one of my socks that was lying there and zipped to the other side where he sat down and gave me one of those "come and get it" looks.

"Lymie, help me catch him, will ya? We gotta get him cleaned off. Sneak around behind him and grab him while he's staring at me."

"Ty, for somebody that's smart, you're pretty dumb. He's still on a leash!"

Lymie slipped the end of the leash off the fence post and started reeling Reginald in. Reginald dug in his heels like a mule, but it was no use; he came skidding across the hood like some kind of a four-legged water skier. I grabbed him. He dropped the sock and started blasting away at my eardrums.

"Lymie, stuff the sock back in his mouth!"

Lymie did it, but Reginald spit it right out and started yapping his lungs out again. Only this time he was nipping at my ears and pulling my hair. I yanked him out in front of me and held him at arm's length.

"Lymie, the sock!"

"He doesn't want it."

"He doesn't *want* it?" I rolled my eyes. Then I pushed Reginald in Lymie's face. "Take him!"

When he did, I grabbed the sock and stuck it back in Reginald's mouth. Before he could spit it out, I cranked both ends around the back of his head and tied them. Reginald bopped his head around like a madman and made a few muffled arfs. The way his eyes were bugging out of his head, I was afraid he'd have a heart attack or something before we got done.

"Come on," I said. "There's a faucet on the side of the clubhouse. We'll rinse him off."

"How we gonna get him dry in time?" Lymie said, trailing after me.

"We won't. His leash is long enough so if we're lucky Mrs. Oster'll just think a sprinkler popped up around him while he was playing on the grass."

There was a hose with a nozzle on it already hooked up to the faucet. I grabbed it and made a few test squirts in the air. Reginald looked at me like he thought I was a psychopath. I don't think he would have made another peep even if I pulled the sock out.

"Okay, Lymie, get him down here. Quick, before we attract a crowd."

As soon as the water hit him, Reginald went stiff as a board. Lymie set him down and he stood there like a coffee table. The mud from his head washed down and turned his chest gray, but I figured I'd have him white again in no time and nobody'd be any the wiser.

Then I heard it. From behind me. First a little gasp. Then a full-fledged scream.

"REGINALD!"

I turned and saw Mrs. Oster tearing down the steps of the clubhouse porch like there was a sniper after her or something. Lymie dropped the leash and Reginald came back to life and took off for Mrs. Oster like a shot. The way he jumped into her arms you'd've thought he'd been on a trampoline.

"Oh, baby, baby, baby!" Mrs. Oster cried. "What have they done to my baby?"

Reginald cranked his head around and glared at us with accusing eyes. Lymie and I just gawked back. There wasn't a whole lot we could say.

Mrs. Oster never said a word to us. She sprinted for her car and peeled out, probably heading for the vet's. Reginald glared back at us through the window. My sock was still wrapped around his head.

I looked at Lymie and he looked at me.

"Timothy Tyler McAllister!"

I looked over and saw Mom. Her face was like one of those angry faces they draw in *Mad* magazine. She pointed to the car. Looking like that and then using my full name? I knew it wasn't good.

"Maybe I'll walk home, Ty," Lymie said.

"Lyman Lawrence!" She pointed to the car again.

We both marched.

The trouble with being practically an only child is that since you're the only kid around, everything you do becomes a big deal. Which is great when it comes to Christmas and birthdays and stuff like that. But when something goes wrong, or you make a little mistake in judgment or whatever, parents with one kid go hyper. They know if anything happens to you, they're out of kids.

Sometimes I wish I was somebody like Toddie Phillips. Toddie's this kid in my homeroom. He has eight brothers and two sisters. There's Ralphie and Bart above him. And there's Frankie, Bobby, Mona, Davy, Lester, Harold, Louise, and the baby below him. I don't even know if the baby's got a name yet. And it's a month old.

So naturally with that many kids running around, Mr. and Mrs. Phillips have had to learn to take things in stride. If they got excited over every little thing their kids did, they'd be dead.

Take something that happened last summer. I'm walking down the sidewalk, and I see the Phillipses' car pulling out onto Main Street. It's one of those big old station wagons that's about seven feet tall with wood on the sides—real wood, not that paste-on plastic stuff—and it's filled to the brim with kids and they're flying around inside like those Lotto balls during a drawing. Anyway, halfway through the turn, the back door—driver's side—pops open, and Toddie does a backward roll out onto the street. I try to yell but nothing comes out except a squeak. Toddie does a couple more rolls before he finally stops. Mr. Phillips slams on the brakes, throws it in reverse, and backs up next to where Toddie is sitting on the pavement.

"Toddie!" he yells. "Get back in the car!"

Toddie stands up, brushes himself off, and looks at the street he was just rolling around on.

"Toddie, hurry up!" Mrs. Phillips yells. "We're gonna be late!"

"Why was you leaning against that door," Mr. Phillips butts in, "when you know that latch don't work. If we was on the highway, you coulda got scraped up pretty good."

"Bart pushed me," Toddie says.

Mrs. Phillips turns around. "Bart, you push your brother out that door again and I'll slam you one!"

And that's it. Mr. and Mrs. Phillips turn back around, the car takes off, and the kids go back to whooping it up, punching each other and hanging out the windows just like nothing ever happened.

If I ever fell out the car door like that, my mom would have a spaz attack. And then she'd have my whole body x-rayed so many times I'd probably glow in the dark for years.

Like I said, sometimes I wish I was somebody like Toddie Phillips. Something as little as getting soaked in October and muddying up some dumb poodle wouldn't even get noticed around his house.

Lymie'd gone home right after we got back from the club. He decided all of a sudden he had things he needed to do at his house.

I was on my own.

I could hear the setup from the top of the stairs. I should have known. Mom's big on the belief that if you just bring problems out in the open and discuss them, you can usually work out some kind of a solution. Only she knew if she sat down alone with me and discussed my problems, it might end up being too much like a mother yelling at some poor kid, which Mom didn't really think worked. So she needed to find somebody to sit in and make it seem more like a discussion group. If my brother were around, she'd've dragged him into this. Same with Mrs. Saunders. Unfortunately for Chuckie, he *was* around. He had just packed up his paint cans for the day and was heading out. I kind of froze in my tracks on the top step and listened as Mom tried to rope him in. I was really hoping he'd be able to hold out.

"He likes you, Chuckie," I heard Mom say. "He looks up to you."

"He likes you too, Ms. L. You're good with him. You don't need me."

The L stands for LaMar, which is my mom's maiden name and the name she went by even when she was married.

"It won't take long, Chuckie," Mom persisted. "And I think it would make a world of difference to bring in another point of view on this."

"What do I know about talking to kids?" Chuckie said. "I wasn't even that great a kid myself."

His voice seemed to be moving toward the front door, which was a good sign. I ducked back toward my room a little so I'd stay out of sight.

"Please, Chuckie," Mom said, catching up to him. "If you *had* been a perfect child, you probably *wouldn't* be much help here, but as it is, Tyler really likes to know what you think about things. You're almost the same age as his brother, and he really *has* come to think of you as a brother." She paused. "I realize this isn't part of your job, Chuckie. I'm asking you this as a friend."

It was quiet for a few seconds. No doorknob turned or anything. I could almost feel Chuckie struggling to come up with a comeback that'd work, but that "I'm asking you this as a friend" thing made it pretty tough.

"You win," Chuckie said finally. "Let's get the show on the road."

I groaned.

I looked at Chuckie sitting there. Chuckie looked back at me. I looked at Mom sitting there. Mom looked back at me. Nobody'd said anything yet. I fidgeted. Chuckie even fidgeted. I wasn't sure if Mom was trying to decide on the best way to start or if she was just building some dramatic tension like she'd do if this were a role she was playing, which maybe it was, kind of.

"Tyler," she said after a while, taking a deep breath, "first maybe you could explain to Chuckie and me whatever possessed you to go into that river in the middle of October with your clothes on." She sat back and made this sweeping gesture with her arm so I'd know the floor was all mine.

I gave a feeble shrug. "Would you be happier if I took my clothes off before I went in?"

"You're right," Mom said. "You're absolutely right. Thank you. The clothes are not the point." Even though she was thanking me, she was giving me this big scowl. "The point is," she continued slowly, "that it was my understanding from the last time we had this kind of talk that you were going to make an honest effort to stay out of trouble."

"But I . . ."

Mom held up her hand—the same hand that'd made the sweeping gesture to give me the floor. "What you did this afternoon showed extremely poor judgment. Extremely poor. Especially considering that you spent the last week sick in bed. And not to mention how you should be extra careful anyway because of your allergies and asthma." She waited. "Well?"

I knew any explanation I gave would sound stupid. I looked at Chuckie for help and he shrugged.

33

"I don't know . . . You know how it is, Mom . . ."

"No, we don't know how it is, Tyler. That's why we're asking you to explain."

She kept saying "we" even though Chuckie hadn't made a peep yet. I figured he wanted to get out of there as much as I did.

"All right, Mom," I said, leaning forward. "I tried to tell you all this in the car, but you were like a crazy person. It's simple. Lymie and I thought we'd wade around a little and try to find those Badoglio heads." I shrugged. "That's the whole story."

"Wading? Is that what you call wading? You were soaked from head to toe. Can you believe this, Chuckie?"

Chuckie tried to look like he couldn't believe it.

"Well," I said feebly, "there was this drop-off . . ."

"Yes?"

"Well, while I was wading around I accidentally stepped off this drop-off and that's how I got so wet. And when I sat on the riverbank, that's where I picked up the mud. It wasn't really anybody's fault."

Mom shook her head. "And what about what you did to that poor little dog? How do you expect me to ever face Mrs. Oster again?"

I felt like I was on firmer ground when it came to that mutt. "He did that to himself, Mom. He saw that I was muddy, and he still climbed right up on me. So we had to clean him off. Even though it wasn't our fault. Only he wouldn't shut up, so that's where the sock came in."

"Tyler McAllister, how could you be so cruel?"

"It wasn't *cruel*, Mom. It isn't like I'd been wearing the sock for three days or something. It was a fresh sock. Besides, that stupid Reginald was biting me and . . ."

"You *know* better than to treat a dog that way. A poor, innocent, dumb animal."

"A poor, innocent, dumb animal? He tried to chew my ears off, Mom! I can't believe you'd stick up for a dog over your own son." I tried to look pathetic.

"Don't you try that game on me, mister! I'm not falling for it. You think all you have to do is aim those blue eyes at me and you'll have it made. That's how you finagled your way out to the club in the first place and don't think I didn't know it, although I should probably have my head examined for giving in to you. And now you expect me to tell Mrs. Oster that you were simply defending yourself from her big, vicious dog?"

It was quiet for a minute. I tried to decide if I should just sit there or if I should say something. It felt funny being stared at with nobody saying anything, so finally I took a chance and opened my mouth. "You know, I'm not sure losing Mrs. Oster as a friend is such a bad thing. Think about it. I mean, I know you're new here and everything, but there's gotta be some ladies around town that are more normal than . . ."

"Stop!" Mom said and held up her hand. "Stop, stop, stop."

I stopped.

"You're doing it again," Mom said, "and it won't work. You always try to confuse the issue. This discussion is not about me, young man, so let's not let the focus drift. We're discussing you and what *you* did."

"All right, Mom." I threw up my arms. "I did something wrong. I admit it. So why don't you just punish me and then we can all forget it?"

"You mean *you* can forget it. I can't forget it because I'm the one who lies awake nights worrying about what you might decide to do next. Tyler, what if you had been swept downstream in the freezing water? What if you had drowned or caught pneumonia?"

"Or both," I said, trying to lighten things up.

"Don't you make jokes about this. This isn't funny. You need to learn to think about consequences." She turned to Chuckie. "Did I tell you how he almost made me run over that poor traffic guard a few weeks ago?"

Chuckie nodded. He probably knew the story by heart. Mom had picked me up after school for my weekly allergy shot. I had finished a soda on the steps while I was waiting for her, and when I hopped into the car, I set the can on the floor, figuring I'd return it next time we stopped at some store. We were zipping around the corner heading for Main Street with Mom asking me the usual questions about how my day went, what I'd learned in school, that kind of thing, when it happened. Instead of waiting ten seconds to let us go by like anybody normal would, this crossing guard, some old retired guy, scooted out in front of us waving his little stop sign. Mom hit the brake. Nothing happened.

"Mom!" I yelled. "You're gonna smear that guy!"

By now Mom was just about standing up in her seat, bearing down on that brake for all she was worth. The car finally stopped less than a yard from the old guy. He hadn't budged. He just stood there scowling at us. And waving the stupid sign in our windshield.

Mom was pretty well shook. She was all white and trembly, and she refused to move the car another foot when the guy waved us on even though cars behind us were honking their horns. "I am not driving a car with no brakes!" she said.

"Hey, Mom—look," I said. I reached down under the brake pedal and came up with my soda can which was scrunched down to half its size. "Your brakes are fine. Here's the problem."

If looks could kill . . . "How . . . do you . . . manage . . . to do . . . these things?" Mom asked through her teeth as we took off.

I got the chicken pox the next day, so except for that first night I didn't get yelled at that much for what had happened. But I knew I was going to hear more about it now.

"Chuckie," Mom said, "did I tell you how he said it was the guard's fault for not getting out of the way?"

Chuckie nodded.

"It's true, Chuckie," I said. "What kind of fool stands around in front of a runaway car? I mean, you give some people a little authority . . ."

Chuckie looked at me. I could see him trying to hide a smirk.

"Besides, some other kid might have chucked the can out the window and littered the street. But I don't do things like that. I've been raised to know better."

That kind of widened Chuckie's smirk a little. I knew if I could make him laugh the meeting would be as good as over.

Mom cleared her throat. "What I'm trying to say, Tyler . . . is . . ." She paused and groped around for the right words.

"You see, Mom. You're not even sure what you're trying to say."

Chuckie almost snickered out loud. Mom gave him the eye.

"What I'm trying to say, Tyler . . . I'm trying to say that you should stop and think before you do things. It's as simple as that. Don't be so impulsive. Think, think, think." She jabbed her finger at my head on each "think."

I looked at her. "So like every time I have an empty soda can I should go into a deep meditation to decide what to do with it?"

Chuckie was taking a sip of coffee and he almost gagged.

"Forget the soda can!" Mom almost yelled. Then she kind of pulled herself together and said quieter, "That was an accident."

"You brought it up, Mom."

"I'm sorry," Mom said. "I take it back. Forget the soda can. Forget the guard. Forget that whole incident."

I shrugged. "Okay, Mom. It's forgotten." I waited a second. "So are we through?"

Chuckie bit his lip and tried to shield his face from Mom. Even Mom seemed pretty close to smiling. Whenever the sides of her mouth start to twitch, I know I've got her.

"Tyler, listen to this," she said. "There are good ideas and there are bad ideas. Most experts would agree that submerging yourself in an icy river in October when you're supposed to be home sick, and gagging someone's dog with a sock, are bad ideas. Tyler, you have intelligence. You have imagination. How can you even *entertain* such foolish ideas?"

"I don't know," I told her honestly. "They don't seem that dumb till after I do them."

"I've got it, Ace," Chuckie said. By now he had given up trying to look serious. "No matter what you decide to do, don't do it. That's the only way you'll be safe."

"You're not helping, Chuckie," Mom said, but I could tell she'd about given up hope of keeping the discussion serious. As a last ditch effort to have some good come out of it, she grabbed my ears and cranked my head around till we were eye to eye. "Tyler, I know you understand what I'm saying. Will you try harder? *Please*?"

"Yeah," I said. "I know what you're saying, Mom. And I'll try harder. I really will."

And I meant it. I really did. Right up until Lymie showed up the next day with another dumb idea. Only it didn't seem so dumb at the time. At least not trouble-causing dumb. It really didn't.

5

Get out here!" Lymie yelled.

No "Hello" or "Good morning" or anything. Just "Get out here." I looked out the kitchen window and wondered what Miss Manners would say about Lymie. It didn't matter. I had a pretty good idea what Lymie would say about Miss Manners.

I ran out to see what the big deal was. Lymie grabbed his bookbag off his handlebars and handed it to me. It almost yanked my arm out of its socket.

"What's in there, Lymie, your lunch?"

He gave me a dirty look. "If you ate like I did, Ty, you might not be so pitiful."

He grabbed the bookbag and lugged it to the garage. I was pretty sure Lymie had picked up some worthless piece of junk from the side of the road, but I'm a sucker for a mystery so I was right at his heels. I watched as he set the bookbag on the workbench and dragged out two huge oval-shaped rocks. He stared at them proudly.

"Well?" he said when I didn't say anything.

"I don't believe it, Lymie. You carried those two jerky-looking rocks all the way from your house? You're worse off than I thought."

"These aren't just rocks, numbnoodle. Look at their shape."

"Very nice, Lymie. They're *oval-shaped* jerky-looking rocks."

"Tyler," he said, all excited, "these rocks are shaped like people's heads!"

"So?"

"So? So if somebody like that Badoglio guy could make money sculpturing, why can't we? We'll chisel a couple of faces on these things and we're in business."

I rolled my eyes. "Be real, Lyme. You're almost flunking eighth grade art."

"Tyler," Lymie said, looking all amazed that anybody could be so dense, "you saw Badoglio's work. That guy wouldn't have even made it *into* eighth grade art! Come on, go get that art book so we can use it for ideas."

"Lymie, this is stupid," I told him. "This is stupid even for you. Let's get out of here and go do something fun. It's a nice day. We oughta be out shooting hoop or something."

I headed for the door. Lymie stepped into my path.

"*My* idea is stupid? After what you did yesterday, you're gonna tell me *my* idea is stupid?"

I thought about that. "Yeah," I said.

Lymie stood there studying me for a minute. I think he was trying to decide if he should belt me. Finally he stepped out of my way.

"Forget it, Ty. If you don't want to help me, don't." He grabbed his bookbag. "Even though I do all *your* dumb stuff . . ."

"Oh, great," I said. "You're gonna get all huffy now."

"Forget it, Ty. Just drop it." He grabbed one of the rocks and stuffed it back in his bookbag. "Just forget I exist."

I took a deep breath and gave a big shrug to the ceiling. "Don't be such a wuss, Lyme. I'll help you already."

Next thing I knew I was running into the house for the modern art book.

40

"Tools," Lymie said. "We need power tools." He scrounged around the workbench. "Like this drill set." He yanked it off the shelf.

I laughed. "You really think you can make some kind of an art treasure with a Black and Decker drill?"

"Why not?" Lymie opened the box.

"Because . . ." I rolled my eyes. "You're supposed to sweat over these things with hammers and chisels and stuff. None of those old artists ever used power tools. They wouldn't have been caught dead . . ."

"Only 'cause they didn't have electricity," Lymie said. "They'd've been jerks to do all that work by hand if they'd had electricity. Just think how many heads Badoglio could've turned out if he'd had one of these things." He waved the drill in my face. "Or one of these." He reached up on the shelf and grabbed a Dremel Variable Speed Moto-Tool kit and a router.

"I don't know if I'm allowed to use any of that," I said. "All that stuff is Chuckie's."

Lymie was busy laying out all kinds of wheels and pads and discs in a neat little row. "Did he ever tell you you couldn't?"

"No."

"All right then." He plugged in the drill. "Besides, I took woodshop in seventh grade. I know how all this stuff works." He stuck a medium-sized bit in, tightened it down, and whirred it in my face a few times. "Hold my rock down, will ya?"

"*Hold* your rock down?"

"You want it to roll all over the place while I'm working on it, lamebrain?" He whirred the drill in my ear.

"Like I might really hold down a rock while you're drilling on it," I said, pushing the drill away.

"You got a better idea?"

"Ever hear of a vise, goofis?" I lugged his rock over to the vise, cranked the jaws as wide as they'd go, and crammed the rock down in it.

41

"Yeah, I heard of a vise. I just didn't know you had one."
Lymie unplugged the drill and plugged it in again next to
the vise. "Be careful you don't scratch it all up."

"Relax, I'll put a cloth around it." I grabbed a greasy red
rag that was lying there, wrapped it around the sides of the
rock as best I could, and cranked down on the handle.

"Okay," Lymie said. "Now sit up there in front of me."

"Why?"

"You can be my model." He said it like it was some big
honor. "Come on. Hurry up."

I groaned. Then clearing off a spot on the workbench,
I hopped up and sat behind the vise, Indian style. "You
want me to smile or be serious?" Like it would make a
difference.

"Doesn't matter right away. First I gotta get the shape of
your head down. But when I get to your face, be serious.
You never see anybody smiling in real art."

He took another look at Badoglio's heads in the book
and then studied my head a little before revving up the
drill. Then, as an afterthought, he set it down, grabbed an
old nail, and began scratching a shape around the outside
of the rock.

"That's supposed to be the shape of my head?" I said,
peering down at it.

"Shut up." Lymie grabbed a hunk of cardboard and braced
it up between me and the rock so I couldn't see what he was
doing anymore.

"You artists are so temperamental."

"Shut up."

I sat around twiddling my thumbs as Lymie drilled away.
Every so often he'd switch bits or stick in a polishing wheel
or grind away with the moto-tool or something. And every
once in a while he'd take a peek at the art book to see how
he was doing. And all the time he was grunting and clicking
his tongue like he does when he gets really involved in
something. It was funny to watch him for a while, but I've
never been one who could sit around for too long. After
about a half hour, I'd had it.

42

"Lymie, aren't you done yet? My legs are falling asleep."

"What do you want me to do about it? Make 'em coffee?" That cracked him up.

"Funny, Lyme. I'm taking a break."

"Geez, Ty, I'm just getting going here."

I stood up and almost collapsed. My left leg was like soft rubber. I had to grab one of the huge floor-to-ceiling beams to keep myself from toppling off the workbench, and I picked up some pretty decent slivers in the act. Lymie was a big help, all hyper about covering up his stupid rock head so I wouldn't get a glimpse of it. Like that's all I had on my mind.

"You know, Tyler," Lymie said, not even noticing that I was hugging the beam over him like some stupid panda bear. "I'm kinda getting into this. I don't think I'd mind being an artist."

I shook my head. Another of Lymie's big career decisions.

"I'm serious," Lymie said. "Check it out. You make your own hours. No dragging yourself out of bed in the morning. You're your own boss."

"Yeah," I said, figuring one of us had to be realistic. "And what if nobody buys any of your stuff?" I rubbed my leg.

"I don't know. Then maybe I'd get a job as an art teacher or something. I'm used to yelling at kids from when I'm home."

"Lymie," I said with all the patience I could muster, "you have to get a license to teach. That means four years of college for a bachelor's degree and another year or two for a master's. You don't just wander into a classroom and start yelling at kids. You gotta be trained."

I was used to having to explain everything to Lymie. Not that he was necessarily dumber than me or anything, although he probably was. It gets back to that only child thing. Since I was the only kid around, Mom and Mrs. Saunders and Christopher and everybody took time to talk things over with me. Like if I said I wanted to be a doctor

43

or something, Mom would get me books about it and tell me how hard I'd have to work and how many years I'd have to go to school—that kind of thing—so I'd grow up being more realistic about what I might end up doing. Lymie's parents had their hands full with his little brothers, Larry and Lonnie, who are a real handful even without adding Lymie and his sister Susan (although she's not that much trouble), so they didn't have time to bother with things like explanations. If Lymie said he wanted to be a doctor, they'd say something like, "That's nice, Lymie," and that'd be it. Lymie probably thought if you wanted to be a brain surgeon, you'd take a six-week course like at Chauffeur's Training School or something.

"I'm not talking about high-school art," Lymie said. "I could teach little kids. All you have to do is teach them to draw houses and trees and stuff. I could handle that."

"Ever hear of psychology, Lymie? If you're going to be stuck in a room with a bunch of little kids, you need to know psychology. Otherwise they'd drive you over the edge in two days." I jumped to the floor and rubbed my leg some more.

"I'd just tell them to sit down and shut up—or else." He waved his fist to demonstrate the "or else."

"Lymie," I said, trying to be patient, "there's no 'or else' anymore. You touch a kid these days and you get sued for about a trillion dollars. A lot of parents are sitting around just waiting for somebody to hit their kid. Nowadays it's psychology or nothing."

Lymie looked puzzled. Even more than usual.

"For example," I said. "Let's say you catch one kid jabbing another kid with his paintbrush. Whaddaya do?"

"I tell him to cut it out or else."

"*Lymie.*" I took a deep breath and reminded myself it wasn't his fault. "There's no 'or else' and the kids know it. Even little kids know their rights. So you have to outsmart 'em. That's the idea behind psychology. You go over and tell the kid who's doing the jabbing how you knew somebody years ago that had his eye poked out by a paintbrush.

44

Then you ask him how he'd feel knowing that he'd blinded a kid for the rest of his life and tell him how he'd have to carry that burden around until the day he died. You show him how two lives can be ruined by one paintbrush."

"But the kid that got jabbed would have one good eye left. His life wouldn't be ruined."

I groaned. Lymie couldn't just learn something from you. He always had to nitpick and try to trip you up.

"Then you say that the kid with one eye couldn't see things in three dimensions and he ended up driving his bike off a cliff or something. You improvise."

"No kid's gonna be dumb enough to believe that."

I knew Lymie pretty well. And I was ready for him.

"Lymie, would you put a tack on somebody's chair?"

"Whaddaya think I'm crazy or something? You can paralyze somebody that way."

I smiled and nodded my head. "See. That's an example of psychology. Every teacher has this fear of sitting on a tack. So they all tell kids this story about some poor slob being paralyzed from sitting on one. See, Lyme, teachers know that there're probably kids who don't like them, but they're banking on the fact that there's not one kid in the class who's mean enough to want to paralyze them. And it works like a charm."

Lymie scrunched up his face, thinking. "So you're saying nobody ever got paralyzed from sitting on a tack?"

"I wouldn't be surprised," I told him. "Teachers always tell that story but they never give names and addresses, do they? And even if it did happen, I bet there are lots of examples of kids who've put tacks on chairs and ended up getting a good laugh out of it, but they don't tell you about that." I studied Lymie as he tried to take all this in. "The point is, Lyme, you don't only teach kids to draw trees and houses and sidewalks. You also gotta learn to control their minds. Otherwise they'll tear the place apart on you."

"Wow," Lymie said, sitting down. "I wonder what else they made up?" He was thinking so hard I half expected to see puffs of smoke rising up from his head.

45

But that's the way Lymie is. You have to tell him stuff that people from smaller families learned when they were little. And when it finally sinks in, he's so amazed.

It all goes back to whether or not your parents had time to teach you anything, although I used to think it was purely biological, and if you were born into a family that already had a lot of kids, there was a good chance you'd be born dumber than an only child. Right off the bat. Like maybe you could only divide up genes so many times and still get a halfway intelligent kid. But then I figured that if dumbness was just a question of worn-out genes, in a family like the Phillipses, the first kids should have been smart and then they should have gradually gotten dumber as you went down the line. But as far as I could tell, all the Phillips kids were equally dumb. At first I played with the idea that maybe Mr. and Mrs. Phillips knew they wanted a lot of kids and were kind of saving themselves so the last ones wouldn't get gypped. But that seemed a little far-fetched, even for a family like the Phillipses. So I started watching how kids from big families were raised. And I noticed that Mr. and Mrs. Phillips barely had time to teach their kids even simple things—like eating with utensils. The kids didn't have a chance.

"Break's over," Lymie said when he got done thinking about teachers and tacks and stuff. "Back on the bench."

I climbed back up and sat there digging out the slivers I'd picked up from the beam. Lymie kept yelling for me to keep my head up so I figured he was putting on the finishing touches. It was pretty boring, but I had to kind of admire Lymie, the way he poured himself into that rock. He'd squint at me, studying, and then go back to whirring away at it like a madman. I even started to think he might be making something important. Before he was done, he'd used about every attachment for both the drill and the moto-tool: bits, sanders, polishing wheels, you name it. I couldn't wait to see the result. I'd never been carved in stone before.

"Done!" Lymie yelled.

Finally.

"Lemme see!" I hopped down, landed on a polishing wheel and almost broke my ankle.

Lymie flattened the cardboard over the head and looked down at me. He was beaming with pride. Never mind that I was rolling around on my back clutching my ankle.

"Tyler, get up. I'm gonna unveil it."

"Well, unveil it then!" I snapped, getting up and testing some weight on my bad ankle. "You always have to make such a big production out of everything." God, my ankle hurt!

Lymie whipped off the cardboard and there the thing sat. I didn't know what to say at first. With the red cloth still hanging out from the sides of its head, it looked more like Bozo the Clown than me. Only it had this kind of puffy, full look around the cheeks and mouth, like the way you look about a half a second before you puke your guts out. I limped in closer and stared at it. It stared back with this dumb expression, like it had been gonged over the head with a lead pipe or something. About the only part of it that might have looked like me was the nose. I've got one of those upturned noses that adults love to tweak. So did it. Except that its nose was quite a bit longer than mine and it was kind of attached to its upper lip.

"Lymie, that thing's pitiful! I can't believe even *you* could make something that ugly!" I started laughing and leaned in to check on it from another angle.

Lymie didn't say a word. He turned away and started putting Chuckie's tools back in their boxes. The way he didn't call me a name, or try to belt me, or slam the tools around, I knew he was pretty hurt. He kept turning so I couldn't get in front of him to see his face. I hoped he wasn't crying. After all, making that head was a big deal to Lymie, and I'd insulted it. Not that there was any getting around it. The thing *was* ugly, and somebody was bound to mention it sooner or later even if I didn't. But Lymie had struggled all afternoon to make it perfect, and it just didn't seem fair.

47

I looked at it again. Then at Lymie. I got an idea.

"Lymie," I said. He didn't look. "I get it now. I see what you did. Pretty smart!" I tried to sound amazed.

"Huh?" Lymie turned around and eyed me suspiciously. Thank God he wasn't crying.

"You remembered what I forgot, Lyme. The best art is always kinda ugly. That's what sells."

"Yeah, Tyler," Lymie said, already starting to soften. "Pretty stuff you can get out of magazines."

"Yeah, look at the *Mona Lisa*. She's pretty ugly."

"That's right," Lymie said. "Even *without* the mustache."

"You're smarter than I thought, Lyme."

"Yeah," Lymie said, thinking about it. "I am." He stepped forward and started admiring the thing all over again, his whole face glowing.

If my face ever gets scarred with acid or something and I can't make a living as an actor, I should go into public relations. I'd have it made.

6

Lymie came back the next day to be the model for my rock. I'd skimmed through the modern art book the night before, but I didn't get any good ideas from it. Since I wasn't seriously planning on making money off my head, I didn't see any reason why mine should have to be ugly.

I had all the tools laid out when Lymie arrived. He climbed up behind the vise where my rock was waiting. I braced up the cardboard, same as Lymie did the day before, so I wouldn't have to listen to his stupid advice. I knew Lymie, and since he'd had one more day's experience than me, I figured he'd be thinking he knew everything.

First I etched out the basic shape of Lymie's head. Even though his face is pudgy, his head is pretty square and I probably could have done a better job by tracing a book or something and then rounding out the corners. But that seemed like cheating. Just using power tools was probably cheating enough. Besides, maybe Lymie didn't even know how square his head was and me tracing around a book might have hurt his feelings. You can say a lot of rotten things to Lymie and it doesn't faze him a bit, but then— bang—out of the blue you can hurt his feelings without

49

even meaning to. Like when I innocently mentioned that his rock had turned out ugly.

A lot of Chuckie's drill bits were already worn down and a few were twisted into funny shapes. His polishing wheels had seen better days too. Which meant that if Lymie *was* able to sell his stupid-looking head, first thing we'd have to do would be to buy Chuckie all new tools. I might even have to try to sell the one I was making. Even though I wasn't planning on making mine ugly enough to be considered real art, somebody might want it.

As soon as I started in, I realized why Lymie had bent some of the bits. The thing was as hard as a . . . I know it sounds stupid to say, but it was as hard as a rock. Luckily it wasn't one of those superhard rocks, like granite or marble. It was more powdery—probably some kind of off-colored limestone—but it was still pretty hard. And you had to chip away a lot of it to make a face. Say, for instance, you wanted the nose to stick out an inch. That meant you had to chip away almost an inch of solid rock from all around the nose. And you couldn't get too carried away because you needed to leave enough rock around it to come up with lips and eyebrows and cheekbones and stuff. Even with power tools, I was starting to work up a sweat. Not to mention some sympathy for Badoglio. He may have made some ugly things, but you had to give him credit for doing all that work by hand.

Sitting around being a model gave Lymie's mind time to wander and, as usual, when Lymie's mind wanders, it got all out of hand. Pretty soon he was coming up with ideas about what we could do with the money if we could find somebody rich who wanted to buy his head.

"The first thing I'd get is a new baseball glove. A good glove that costs a couple hundred dollars like the ones they use in the pros." He stopped and thought a minute. "That way when I get into high school, I'll have a better chance of making first string."

"It takes more than a new glove to make first string," I told him. "It takes somebody that knows how to use it."

"Don't worry about me. I know how to use a glove. Mosta the errors I made last summer were because of my old glove. That glove doesn't snag grounders worth beans."

"Right, Lyme," I sneered. I was a little tired of hearing Lymie blame all his errors on his old glove. Lymie had two basic fielding excuses: bad bounces and bad glove. To hear him talk, if he got a new glove and had a smooth playing field, nothing, but nothing, would ever get by him again. Lymie refused to recognize human error when the human he was talking about was him.

By the time I got to the mouth, Lymie was daydreaming about all kinds of new stuff: a new tennis racket, a hockey stick, a ten-speed bike—and all of it was top of the line. Finally, I'd heard enough.

"Get outta here, Lymie," I said. "You're gonna make all that money off that head?"

"Duh!" Lymie said. "I'm not talking about just *one* head, Tyler. With everybody in town all excited about art because of this Badoglio celebration, anything artistic is gonna really be in demand. And Lymie-angelo here plans on cashing in."

"Seems like a lot of work to me," I said, "even if anybody *did* want to buy those things." I was trying to polish a zit off my head's forehead, but all the polishing wheels were pretty well spent, so I decided to leave it there. People would just think my model had a zit. Or better yet, I could tell everybody it was one of Lymie's leftover chicken pox scabs.

"I was thinking, Ty. You could probably end up doing a lot of this work by robot. Like if you could come up with one head that a lotta people wanted to buy, you could get one of those computerized robots to turn out a bunch of 'em. You'd be able to crank those things out day and night."

"Right, Lyme," I said. "And when it wasn't busy making heads, we could get it to clean our rooms and do our homework." I laughed.

51

"You know, you're supposed to be smart, Tyler, but sometimes you're pretty dumb. They use robots now to build everything: cars, airplanes, other robots, you name it. You can program a robot to do almost anything you want."

"All right, Lymie. So who's gonna program it? You don't just tell the thing to make a head and then go fishing."

Lymie rolled his eyes. "Tyler, you buy the robot and it's got these things kinda like arms, and they have sensors on them. So all you probably gotta do is have these arms feel around the head you already made, and the sensors send the information to a computer, and the computer memorizes the size and shape and everything else it needs to know and stores it all in its chips. After that, all you'd have to do is see that it's got the right tools and keep it supplied with rocks."

I shook my head. Lymie always gets these big ideas. But it was kind of neat to think about. In fact, I was wishing I had a robot or something to finish off my rock right then. My hands were almost too tired to hold the tools anymore. And even after all the work I'd done, my rock was almost as ugly as Lymie's. It looked kind of like the boogieman in *Friday the Thirteenth*, mask and all. And the more I chiseled away at it, the worse it got. Finally, I called it quits.

"All right, Lymie," I said. "I'm done."

Lymie jumped off the bench and took a peek.

"Hey, Tyler, not bad. That's uglier than mine even."

"Yeah," I said with a sigh. "That's what sells."

I took my head out of the vise and Lymie dug his head out from under the counter, and we set them side by side and studied them. Mine had bags under its eyes and a nose that was too long. But the polishing wheels were too worn to get rid of the bags, and I was afraid if I tried to chisel the nose down to a decent size, the whole thing might break off. Lymie's head still looked like it was thinking about throwing up.

We stared at them for a while, not saying anything.

"Hey, what's the big attraction?"

Lymie and I both jumped about a foot. Then I pushed the cardboard over the heads and turned around. Chuckie was walking our way. We stood there looking like some huge bug had just flown down our throats.

"You guys trying to hide something?"

Lymie and I scrunched closer together and leaned back on the cardboard so Chuckie couldn't see anything. We weren't ready for critics yet.

All of a sudden Chuckie's jaw dropped down. "My tools!" He pushed his way in between us and picked up a couple of broken and twisted-up bits off the floor. "You wrecked my tools!" He stood up and looked at us like we'd just shot his mother or something.

Lymie and I gawked back at him. I gulped. Then I heard Lymie gulp. Chuckie's pretty tough and he could break us both in half if he wanted to.

"Chuckie, don't worry," I stammered. "We're gonna pay you back for your tools."

"You better believe you're gonna pay me back for them! And who told you you could use them anyway?"

"Look, Chuckie," Lymie said, kind of waving his hands for Chuckie to settle down, "we *are* gonna pay you back. We're gonna sell these things we made and make a lotta money." He whipped the cardboard off our heads.

Chuckie stopped glaring at us and started glaring at our rocks. I held my breath and watched him. His scowl disappeared. Then he looked confused. And within ten seconds he was laughing his head off.

"What's so funny?" Lymie said. "It's art. It's supposed to be ugly."

"Yeah," I said. "You think you could do better?"

Chuckie tried to answer a couple of times, but his laughing got the better of him and he couldn't say a word. I looked at Lymie. He looked like he'd been punched in the stomach.

"They're not *that* funny," I said, but it didn't help any.

Chuckie was holding his side now and his face was all twisted and kind of a purple color. He tried to speak a few more times but couldn't.

"Something like this could be worth money," Lymie said in this strange, quiet voice.

"It's happened before," I said and held up the modern art book.

This nearly sent Chuckie into convulsions. He looked like his sides might split. Tears were pouring out his eyes.

There's two kinds of laughter. There's the kind that does your heart good to see, and there's the kind Chuckie was doing then. Lymie and I were glaring at *him* by that time, both of us wishing we'd kept the heads secret and let him keep hollering at us or belt us or something.

"You . . ." he gasped, "you guys . . . ha, ha, ha . . . you guys weren't actually thinking about *selling* those things?"

"Maybe," I said. Then for Lymie's benefit I added, "Maybe we still will."

"That thing . . ." Chuckie said, pointing at my head (the head I made, that is), "that thing could be a mold for a Halloween mask!" He sighed and let out a few leftover chuckles. He wiped his eyes and when he looked up, he saw our stony eyes beading into him. "Seriously, guys . . . I don't mean to be cruel, but I think you'll be paying for my tools out of your allowances. Nobody in his right mind would buy those things."

"Yeah, and what do you know about art?" I said.

Lymie didn't say anything. I knew that wasn't good.

"Look," Chuckie said, "I can't let you guys do this to yourselves. I know you worked hard on these things." He glanced over at a few more of his tools. "You *had* to have worked pretty hard to wreck that much stuff. But you don't want to try to sell those things. You'll get laughed out of town."

Neither of us said anything. But I for one stopped glaring at Chuckie and started eyeing the floor. Lymie probably did too.

"Look, guys," Chuckie said, "I'm sorry I laughed but . . ."

He looked at the heads again. "But you don't want to sell them. Believe me."

We didn't say anything.

"Come on, guys. Lighten up. It's a beautiful day. You're young. You've got your health. If anybody should be mad, it should be me."

"Yeah, right, Chuckie," I said, looking up and giving him another good glare.

Lymie kept quiet. He turned around and picked up his head and put it under the counter. Then he put my head next to his and covered them both with the cardboard. And before I knew it he'd walked out without saying a word.

"I'm sorry, Ace," Chuckie said. "I didn't mean to hurt anybody's feelings. I didn't know those things meant so much to you guys."

"Don't worry about it," I said. "We knew they were ugly."

We saw Lymie go past the open door on his bike.

"You think he'll be all right?" Chuckie asked.

"He'll get over it," I said. "You know Lymie. He always gets these big ideas."

I left the garage and walked toward the house. I don't know why, but I was feeling pretty lousy myself.

7

Chuckie had dinner with us that evening like he usually does on Sunday, and all through it he kept apologizing for laughing at the heads and I kept telling him to forget it. I know *I* wanted to. I felt pretty sorry for Lymie, but I also felt pretty stupid that I'd actually started thinking we might be able to sell those ugly heads too. Plus I must have been getting a little paranoid, because after I left the table, I sat on the stairs around the corner and eavesdropped. I could hear Chuckie mumbling, and a couple of times I heard Mom giggle. My own mother! Then I heard her say, "Oh, that is *so* cute! The poor kids."

Yuck. I had to get out. Talk about wanting to barf.

I spotted the kid before he spotted me. He came shuffling down the sidewalk toward my driveway with his scruffy head sticking out of this old army jacket that was so baggy you had to practically guess the rest of the kid was in there. His hands were crammed deep into his pants pockets, and he looked like a miniature wino or something. I knew it had to be one of the Phillips kids. And judging from his size, he was probably in about the Harold-to-Lester range.

I stepped out into the light. He spotted me and almost jumped.

"Hi, Ty-wer," he said with this big toothless grin. "What aw you doing here?"

It was Lester. Even before he lost his front teeth, he had trouble with my name.

"I live here, Lester. What about you?" He was pretty little to be out on his own. He couldn't have been more than six.

"Wow!" Lester said. "You gotta big house." He jumped up and stretched out his arms the way cheerleaders do at the end of a cheer. Strolling under the archway, he stared down the long driveway, leaning his head forward like a pitcher looking for a sign from his catcher.

"You wiv there awone, Ty-wer?"

"Naw," I said. "My mom lives there, and our house-keeper, only she's away, and sometimes my brother. And over there is the cottage where Chuckie lives. He takes care of the place." I waited while Lester studied the yard. "You didn't tell me what you're doing here all by yourself."

"We went out to get ice cweam at Stewutz," he said, as if that explained the whole thing.

"Yeah, so you were at Stewart's?" I said, knowing he meant the Stewart's ice cream shop back on Main Street. "So what happened to the rest of your family?"

"I hadda go to the baffwoom and they weft."

"They left?" That shouldn't have surprised me. It sounded like something the Phillipses would do. They probably didn't even notice Lester was missing until they got home. "Come on in and we'll call them, Lester. They're probably worried."

"Okay," Lester said and followed me. I could see him out of the corner of my eye trying to step right where I stepped. I smiled. That's the way I used to follow Christopher around.

"Hey, Mom! Chuckie! Look what I found."

They were still at the dining room table finishing their

coffee. Lester grabbed my shirttails and hid behind me. I yanked him around front so they could see. "It's Lester Phillips. His family took off from Stewart's without him."

Mom hopped up and ran over to Lester. I could see Chuckie trying not to laugh.

"You poor thing!" Mom said, leading him to the table and sitting him down. "You must have been scared to death."

"Yeah." Lester shrugged. "I guess I stayed too wong in the baffwoom."

"Don't you worry, Lester. You're all right now," Mom said.

"I'm aw wight now," Lester said.

"I'll call his house," I said and grabbed the phone.

"So, Lester," Chuckie said, "can I get you a beer or anything?"

"Chuckie," Mom said. "Don't tease the poor tyke."

"Ice cweam!" Lester yelled.

Chuckie went to the freezer and grabbed a box of chocolate ice cream and opened it at the table. Lester hung over it like a dog over its dish.

Mrs. Phillips answered the phone and I told her not to worry, that I'd found Lester.

"Lester?" she said. "Where'd you find Lester?"

I told her.

"Stanley!" she yelled while her mouth was still right up against the phone. "We left Lester in town." She said it like you'd say you'd forgotten to get milk at the store. She thanked me though, and said Mr. Phillips would be right in to pick him up.

The three of us sat around watching Lester work on his bowl of ice cream. He held his spoon like a toy shovel, and his face was already pretty smeared up before I got off the phone. It's like little kids are never quite sure where their mouth is and they have to feel around with their spoons to find it.

Lester raised his eyes and watched us watching him. If

he wasn't used to all that attention, at least it didn't affect his appetite.

Pretty soon the phone rang and it was Mrs. Phillips. They couldn't get their car going. The battery was dead or something and the kids were all pushing it around the yard. She said they'd be in as soon as they got it started.

"Hey, Mom," I said. "Their car won't start. Why don't we keep Lester here tonight?"

"I can drive him home," Mom said. "He has school tomorrow and he'll need his school clothes." She looked down at Lester's raggedy clothes.

"These aw my school cwothes." He had finished his ice cream and now he was jumping on the chair. "I want to stay wiff Ty-wer! Pweeze!"

Mom finally gave in and said all right. How could she say no to that grungy little face? Mrs. Phillips said thanks. Three or four times.

"Listen, Lester," I said when we got upstairs. "You can either have Chris's room all to yourself . . ." I motioned left. "Or you can stay in my room with me." I motioned right.

"Your woom!" Lester yelled, jabbing his finger in my face. "I want to stay wiff you."

Mom came up and suggested maybe Lester would like to take a bath. Lester yelled, "A baff! Yeah, a baff!" and started jumping around.

I didn't get that right away. It seemed to fly right in the face of everything I knew about little kids. But I was kind of relieved. If he was going to climb into my bed, which he'd have to since Chuckie'd already taken the extra bed down . . . well, a bath wouldn't hurt.

I ran some water in the tub and passed Lester's clothes out to Mom, so she could throw them in the washer. They must have been on Lester for about a million years. You could almost see fumes coming out of them. Lester needed a bath worse than any kid I'd ever seen. His skin was streaked with all different shades of brown and black and gray. He looked like he'd been tie-dyed. I went to Mom's

59

bathroom, grabbed some bubblebath, and poured in double what it said on the box. Lester stood on the toilet seat watching it bubble. He was singing. You'd think taking a bath was the best thing in the world.

"Tell me something, Lester." I set him in the tub. "Do you get this excited whenever you take a bath?"

"We don't got no bafftub."

I couldn't believe it. I poured in more bubble bath.

Since this was such a big event in Lester's life, I went to my closet and dug out all my old bath toys. You know, rubber ducks, boats, that kind of thing. I hadn't used them in years. You get to a certain age and you take showers. But I'm kind of a pack rat, and Mom kind of gets a kick out of seeing my old stuff. I figured Lester would get a charge out of it too. Besides, I didn't want Lester to get bored until the water'd had a chance to soak through all those layers of grunge.

I squished Lester around and dunked him a bunch of times to get him good and clean. He was having the time of his life and was howling with joy. After about twenty minutes, I pulled the plug and yanked him out because I didn't want him to wrinkle up too bad. You probably shouldn't overdo it your first time.

I wrapped Lester up in a giant bath towel and led him back to my room. Mom was scrounging around for some of my old clothes that might fit him until his clothes came out of the dryer. Lester started jumping on my bed. He'd jump as high as he could twice, then land on his butt, and fly back to his feet. Mom didn't even yell. Each time he came up, he'd be wearing less of the towel. Then one time he flew up and the towel didn't even bother. It just stayed on the bed. Lester didn't even seem to notice. It's funny how little kids are. They couldn't care less if somebody's mother is in the room and their towel falls off.

Mom didn't let on she noticed anything strange, and handed me this pair of jeans I'd outgrown a couple of years ago. I stuck them on Lester and rolled up the cuffs. Mom handed me this old pair of suspenders I wouldn't be caught dead in, and I clipped them to the waist and strung them over Lester's shoulders. When I got done tightening them, the waistband of the jeans was up around his armpits. It didn't matter though. I covered him in a T-shirt that went down to his knees.

When I went back to the bathroom to get a hairbrush, I spotted it—the most humongous bathtub ring I'd ever laid eyes on. It wasn't even in the same league with the dinky little rings I used to get yelled at for leaving. This ring was three dimensional, the kind of ring you'd have to chip off if it ever dried. Even the toys had little rings around them. Being Lester's host, I should have cleaned it off, but I didn't. Not that I wanted to embarrass Lester or anything. But I wanted Mom to see it and feel guilty for all the times she hollered about my little rings.

Back in my room, Mom was putting Lester in socks.

"Mom," I said, "why don't you go and grab some aftershave? Remember how when I was little, Chris used to always put some of that on me after I took a bath?"

"Why that's a nice idea, isn't it, Lester?"

"Aftershabe!" Lester said.

I knew it was a rotten thing to do, but I was afraid Mom would miss seeing that bathtub ring. After a couple of showers, it might start to erode. And I don't know, I wanted her to see it in all its glory. Sometimes parents don't realize how good they have it.

Mom came out a few minutes later with the aftershave and watched as I patted some on Lester's face. But not a word about the ring.

"Hey, Mom," I said, figuring Lester wouldn't mind, "did you check out that bathtub ring?"

"I guess I didn't notice," Mom said.

"Are you kidding, Mom? That thing was massive!"

"I said I didn't notice, Tyler." She was smiling, but it was one of those "How could you say such a thing?" smiles.

When I took the brush and the aftershave back, I took one last peek. It was gone. Vanished. Kaput. I walked up

61

to the tub. Even the toys were clean. I wished I'd taken a picture.

Next I had to come up with things to do that might entertain a little kid and still not bore me too bad. First I took him out to watch the bug zapper. He got a big kick out of it like I knew he would. He jumped around and clapped his hands every time a bug got zizzled.

"He's smokin'!" he'd yell. "That one weally got fwied!"

"You should see it in the summer," I said proudly. "That thing really lights up in the summer." I promised to invite him over next summer to see a real bug-killing display. Lester said he was going to put a bug zapper on his Christmas list.

Next I brought him to the garage to show him the heads. Actually I wanted to look at them again myself and see if they were as bad as Chuckie thought. Plus I kind of wanted to get someone else's reaction, even if it was a little kid's. I dug the heads out and set them on the counter. They looked about the same as I remembered them.

I looked at Lester. He seemed interested. And he didn't laugh.

"I made that one, Lester." I pushed him forward.

He reached out and felt around its face.

"Pwitty good, Ty-wer." He scrunched up his face and peered at both heads from every possible angle. "Yours is the best one."

Lester wanted to bring it in the house and drag it around like a teddy bear or something. I tried to talk him out of it. I said I was afraid he'd drop it on his foot, which was true, but also I didn't want Chuckie to see it again.

"You can carwey it, Ty-wer. We can put it to bed. Pweeze."

"Oh, all right, Lester. If it'll make you happy." I'm easy. I picked up the head and lugged it toward the house, expecting Chuckie to pop up behind me any minute. We made it all the way up to my room without being spotted. Lester ran into Chris's room and grabbed an extra pillow from his bed. Then he put the head in the pillow, set it on my bed, and pulled the covers up around its chin. He even wadded up the blankets to make it look like it had a body. Then he hopped into bed next to it even without being told. The kid was like no other kid I've ever seen.

"Tell us a storwee, Ty-wer."

I felt a little foolish telling a story to these two faces peeping out from the covers, but I did it. When it comes to storytelling, I'm kind of a natural. I told him the "Goldilocks and the Three Bears" story, only in my version Goldilocks was a karate expert, and when the three bears came home and started giving her a hard time, she mopped up the cabin with them. But then they all became friends and the bears told Goldilocks to drop by anytime she wanted. Goldilocks would have invited them over to her place too, except she figured her parents wouldn't want three bears sitting around on all their furniture because they'd probably shed.

"Wow!" Lester squealed, his eyes all bugged out. "That's the best storwee. She flattened them bears, didn't she, Tywer? Pow!"

"Yeah, but only in self-defense," I told him. I didn't want to warp his mind or anything.

"Who's your friend, Lester?"

I jumped. It was Mom. I wondered how much of the story she'd heard.

"Ty-wer." Lester jabbed his finger in my face.

"I meant your other friend." Mom pointed to the goofy rock which was staring up at her from the pillow. I wanted to crawl into a hole and die.

"Ty-wer's head that he made."

I stole a peek at Mom's face. I couldn't tell what she was thinking, but at least she didn't crack up.

"Ty-wer can do anything," Lester said. "Can't you Ty-wer?" He patted my arm.

I hated to let the kid down, but I couldn't very well say yes in front of Mom. It's hard to be a hero in front of someone that used to change your diapers.

"He *is* pretty special," Mom said, and then leaned down and kissed me. Then she kissed Lester. "Lights out. School day tomorrow."

Before she left she gave me a funny look, kind of a little smile mixed with a nod. I don't know. Maybe that bathtub ring made her stop and think after all.

8

I didn't see Lymie till noon the next day. Which was strange. Lymie's the kind of guy that appears out of nowhere, showing up at your locker, or popping up behind you in the hall, or sneaking in ahead of you in the cafeteria line. He always finds me even if I change my routine and go to the library instead of the cafeteria or something. But this time I had to run around looking for *him*. I found him sitting by himself in the far corner of the cafeteria.

"Lymie, where you been? I thought you died or something." I plunked my tray down across from his.

He didn't say anything. He didn't even look up.

"You still upset?"

He stared at his tray.

"Chuckie's sorry about laughing at your head, Lyme."

"I don't want to talk about it, Tyler."

So I changed the subject. I told him about Lester's bathtub ring.

"Big deal," Lymie said. "That kid could leave a ring around a pond." He still didn't look up.

I stared at him for a while.

"Lymie," I said finally, "you gotta snap outta this. This is crazy."

He sat there.

"Hey, Lyme, you remember what this Friday is?"

No answer.

"It's Halloween, that's what. You don't want to be depressed for Halloween, do you? Huh?"

I thought bringing up Halloween might do it. I knew how he'd been saving eggs and tomatoes and stuff since before we got the chicken pox so they'd be good and rotten by Halloween night.

He sighed. I thought that might be a good sign.

"You know what I wanna do, Lyme? I wanna bombard that crossing guard's house. You know, the old guy Mom almost ran over. We'll have to find out where he lives."

No reaction. I might as well have been talking about social studies homework or something. I spotted Mary Grace Madigan and waved her over, figuring maybe she could cheer Lymie up. Mistake. Major blunder. She was with Babette Flosdorf. Babette had a personality like a pit bull, and for some reason she disliked me even more than she did the rest of the world. I groaned.

"Hi, Tyler. Hi, Lymie," Mary Grace said, setting her tray down.

"Shove over, worm," Babette said and plopped down next to me. You could feel the bench sag.

When most people hear the name "Babette," they probably get this picture of a dainty little dark-haired girl, or maybe some sexy lady wearing a flimsy dress in one of those steamy French films you see on cable late at night. I guarantee they don't picture Babette Flosdorf.

"Lymie's depressed," I said to Mary Grace.

"Oh, Lymie, what's the matter?" Mary Grace said.

You could hear Lymie let out this big sigh. But that was it.

"Well," I said, "this weekend we . . ."

"Shut up, Tyler," Lymie said.

I looked at him. "Lymie, you don't have to be so miserable to everybody."

"He's not being miserable to everybody," Babette said. "He's being miserable to you."

"Who's talking to you?" I said, blowing up my cheeks and making a fat face at her.

Mary Grace kicked me under the table.

"I'd be depressed too if I had a friend like you," Babette said.

"Which you don't," I said.

We glared at each other without blinking for like two minutes. Finally she turned to Lymie.

"So what's the problem, Lymie?"

Talk about not being able to take a hint.

"He *said* he didn't want to talk about it, Ba*boon*."

Babette hissed at me. I swear to God she hissed. And she made this fist and stuck it in my face so close I had to cross my eyes to look at it. "Say one more word," she said. "Go ahead. Make my day."

I turned to Mary Grace. Not that I was scared of Babette. I was pretty sure I could take her if I had to, but I knew how idiotic I'd look rolling around the cafeteria floor with some fat girl who thought she was Clint Eastwood.

"Just like I thought," Babette said and grabbed her tray. "You're a chicken." She left.

"Oowuuu! Oooowuuuuuu!" I yelled. It was as close to a moose call as I could come. "Babette, your mother's calling!" I pushed my chair back and got ready to make tracks in case she came back. She didn't.

"Satisfied?" Mary Grace said.

"Oh, like that was my fault," I said. "Like she didn't start in on me first or anything."

"Only because she thinks you don't like her."

I snorted. "I don't like her, Mary Grace. How could I? She's like an attack dog. A fat one."

"You *could* make an effort," Mary Grace said. "She thinks you're conceited because you never talked to her when you started school here."

"Mary Grace, I never talked to anybody when I first got here. I don't talk much until I get to know people."

"Well, Babette thinks that because you moved here from Los Angeles and because your mother and brother are in the movies, you think you're too good for everybody."

"That's her problem," I said. "How come you don't think I'm conceited? Or do you?"

"Of course not. But Babette is very sensitive."

"Sensitive!" I practically squeaked. "You gotta be kidding!"

"Yes, sensitive. Especially about her weight, which you go out of your way to mention every time you see her."

"Well, she's got enough of it to be sensitive about."

"There. See what I mean? You make one crack after another about her little weight problem. Why do you have to be so mean?"

"A *little* weight problem? She's like a genetic engineering experiment that went bad." I looked at Lymie to see if that got a smile. It didn't. I looked back at Mary Grace. I didn't get one there either.

"Tyler, *that* was cruel." She picked up her tray and left.

"Boy, Lymie," I said. "Some days . . ."

"Forget it, Ty. I'm not in the mood." He picked up his tray and left.

I was all alone. I wanted to cry. Some days it seems like the whole planet has gotten up on the wrong side of the bed.

Lymie pedaled up to my house that evening. His bookbag was slung over his handlebars. I was on the porch doing my homework. Or trying to. It was pretty hard to concentrate after the kind of day I'd had.

"Get your bike, Tyler."

At least Lymie was back to normal—giving orders and not even saying hello.

"Why?" I asked.

He didn't answer. He ducked inside the garage. I went around back to get my bike, hoping Mom wouldn't see me because I knew she'd never let me leave right before dark. When I got back, Lymie was loading his head into his bookbag.

"Where's your head, Tyler?"

"It's in the . . ."

"Get it."

I ran to get it. I bet I was a slave in some previous life. The rock was still on my bed with the covers wrapped around its neck, or they would have been if it had a neck. Mom had made my bed, which was strange in itself, and she'd left the head right there. I wondered if she'd dragged Chuckie up there to laugh at it again. Probably not. I think she'd developed more of an appreciation of me after seeing the way Lester lived.

I ran into Chuckie as I was sneaking out the back door. He smirked when he saw what I was carrying.

"What are you gonna do, Ace? You gonna sell those things after all?"

"No, we're *not* gonna sell them," I said, slipping past him. I don't trust Chuckie when he gets that certain gleam in his eye.

"Well, if you do," he said, "make sure you sell them together as a set."

"Why?" I stopped and eyed him suspiciously.

"You know what they say, Ace. Two heads are better than one."

That cracked him up. I could still hear him har-harring after I went around the corner. I even had to kind of smile myself.

Lymie stuffed my head into his bookbag and pedaled away without saying a word. I took off after him. I knew if Mom saw me, she'd forget all about how I didn't leave bathtub rings or jump up and down on my bed anymore, and she'd be back to yelling at me again. But I couldn't help it. Lymie was up to something, and I didn't want to miss it.

Ten minutes later we were slipping and sliding down the embankment behind Badoglio's house. I didn't need to be

69

a genius to figure out what Lymie had in mind. And I didn't like it.

"Lymie, something tells me we're asking for trouble."

"Hey, aren't you the one who was all excited about Halloween today? Well, just consider this the beginning of our Halloweening. Our first prank of the season."

I stopped and looked at him. "Lyme, you realize practically the whole town is going to be here when they dredge . . ."

"Hyper down, Ty. It's a joke. A little joke. They'll drag the things up, everybody'll have a little laugh, and that'll be that. We keep our mouths shut and they'll never even know who did it."

Looking at it that way, it did seem kind of funny. What the heck. We both got a running start and shot-putted our heads as far out into the water as we could. Lymie's went twice as far as mine. I was afraid if I got carried away, I'd fall in and then I'd never be able to go home again. We stood there for a minute after they disappeared. By then it was almost dark.

"We better hit the road, Tyler. My parents don't even know I'm gone."

"Hey, Lymie," I said as we climbed the embankment to get our bikes. "I hope they find them both together."

"Why?"

"You know what they say," I said. "Two heads are better than one."

"You're really stupid, Tyler. You know that."

There was just enough light left so I could see Lymie's lips trying not to break into a smile. Probably his first smile of the day.

9

I love Halloween. You don't have to wear good clothes, or visit relatives, or sit through any big dinner. And you get to dress however you want and act like an animal. In fact, on Halloween adults expect kids to act like animals. Not that they like it or anything. They try to fight back by setting up an "organized activity" like a dance or a party, so they can herd the kids into one place and keep them surrounded. But that usually works against them. If it weren't for the stupid activity, a lot of our parents wouldn't even let us out of the house. And the funny part is, the only kids that end up staying at those things are the ones who wouldn't get in trouble anyway.

After Lymie and I chucked our heads into the river, he cheered up enough so he could do some serious thinking about Halloween.

"Tyler," he said the next morning, "this year we're gonna get the Keepouts."

My jaw dropped down. I felt a tingle go up my spine. I couldn't believe it.

*   *   *

Up until then the Keepouts were more like a legend to me than real people. They were the kind of people you'd talk about late at night when you wanted to be scared, but not too scared. Like the way kids talk about *The Texas Chainsaw Massacre*—half laughing, but half not laughing.

The Keepouts lived in a creepy old house on the corner of Elm and Maple, across from the back side of Academy Park. They moved to Wakefield a couple of months before we did. They used to live in Boston or someplace, but they said there was too much crime there and that the cops wouldn't do a thing about it. Which may have been true for all any of us knew. But the funny thing is, a few weeks after they settled in Wakefield, they started saying there was too much crime *there* too and that the Wakefield cops were as bad as the Boston ones. Like if they saw a group of kids heading for Buster's Game Room or coming home from football practice or something, they'd call the police and report how they'd just spotted some gang activity and how the police'd better break it up. And it didn't even have to be a group of kids. They'd report anybody they thought looked suspicious, which turned out to be almost everybody. So it didn't take the police long to get really fed up with them. Or the kids either.

By the time we moved to Wakefield, the Keepouts had already started putting up signs all around their property. First there were signs like "KEEP OUT" and "NO TRESPASSING." Simple things. Then they started getting more involved, and you'd start seeing things like "ENCROACHERS BEWARE AT ALL TIMES" and "PROCEED ON PREMISES AT YOUR OWN RISK." One day they even stuck out this sign that said, "YES, THIS MEANS YOU!" Plus they cranked out about twenty more "KEEP OUT" signs. Which is how they got their name. I didn't even know what their real name was since nobody ever used it. Even adults called them the Keepouts.

By late summer their place was so plastered with signs, it became kind of a tourist attraction. You'd always see cars stopped out in front checking out the signs. They even did a piece on the Keepouts for the TV news. Mrs. Keepout got on camera and said how Buster's Game Room was engaged in drug trafficking and that rock concerts should be banned from the Saratoga Performing Arts Center because kids went there to worship the devil. Then Mr. Keepout said that since the police wouldn't protect anybody, it was up to each family to protect itself. He said he intended to do just that.

Except for that news show, I had never even seen the Keepouts. They must have left home sometimes to get groceries and stuff, but I never saw them. Whenever I walked past their house, I always had that creepy feeling that I was being watched. Like they were lurking behind the curtains or something. Some of the kids told stories about how Mr. Keepout would hide behind his signs and jump out and grab kids if they walked too close to his yard. And Toddie Phillips told me once how he'd seen Mr. Keepout walking around the yard with a loaded gun. I don't know how Toddie could've known the gun was loaded, but he swears it was.

Myself, I figured the Keepouts probably weren't even that dangerous. They just wanted to scare everybody away. And it worked. I never once walked by their place at night. I never even thought about it. Until now.

Halloween was on a Friday night which was good because we could stay out later, but I was glad it wasn't the thirteenth.

Lymie showed up at seven thirty, and we went up to my room to go over the details of the attack.

"Okay, Ty, what kind of stuff you got to throw?"

He knew perfectly well what kind of stuff I had to throw. Nothing. Because he knew I had to promise Mom I wouldn't waste anything edible because of all the starving people in the world. Besides, it was a fact that Lymie had enough tomatoes and eggs and things for both of us. And it was kind of a technicality, but by Halloween Lymie's stuff wouldn't be edible any more, so I could chuck it without feeling guilty.

I went into Chris's cabinet and grabbed a can of shaving cream. Just so I'd have something to show him.

"Real good, Ty," Lymie sneered. "You're lucky you got me around to take care of you, you know that?"

I sighed. I knew that's what he'd been waiting to say.

"Okay," Lymie said, "first we go to the school . . ."

"The school?" I whined. "You mean we're going to that stupid dance? Why?"

"Two reasons," Lymie said. "The first is food. They'll have tons of it and there's no reason we shouldn't get some."

"I don't know," I said. "It seems kinda like stealing or something. You know, to eat their food and then not stick around to bob for apples or anything."

"Tyler . . ." Lymie paused and shook his head. He looked confused. Or maybe disgusted. "You're probably the only kid in the whole entire world who'd even think of something like that. Does your mother make you bob for apples and stuff before she feeds you?"

"No."

"All right then. Shut up and listen. The second reason we go to the dance is so you can tell your mother you're going there without getting that stupid look you always get when you try to tell a lie."

That was true. I was the worst liar in the whole world. Especially around my mother. And especially when she suspected something, which she would, since it was Halloween.

"Okay," I said, "so we go to the dance, eat, and then leave and pelt the Keepouts' house with eggs and stuff."

"Tyler," Lymie said. "We're not just pelting the Keepouts' house. We're pelting the Keepouts."

I gulped. "Are you kidding me?" I had pictured us running down the street at like ninety miles an hour and letting everything fly. "You didn't tell me that. You want to get us shot or something?"

"It wasn't my idea," Lymie said. "But there's no way we can get out of it now."

74

"Why not? Whose stupid idea was it anyway?"

"Babette Flosdorf's. And she's telling everybody that you're gonna chicken out."

I groaned.

Mom stopped us at the front door. I was wearing my raggy old army jacket. It wasn't a costume or anything, just something with huge pockets and I didn't have to worry about it getting ruined.

"Hi, Mom," I said, forcing a smile.

"Hi, Mrs. LaMar," Lymie said.

"Hello, boys." Mom folded her arms and looked us over. "Nice jacket, Tyler. Nice big pockets." She rapped on the side of one of my pockets and you could hear a muffled tin sound.

"It's shaving cream, Mom. Not food."

"I don't like it," she said. "It's wasteful."

"Aw, Mom," I whined, "it's not like it's food or anything. I mean, are you going to tell me there are people running around Asia with beards because of me?"

She smiled. A little. And she grabbed my collar.

"You're going to the dance," she said.

I nodded.

"You'll behave yourself and be home by ten-thirty."

I nodded.

"Or else."

I nodded.

As soon as we got outside, Lymie said, "Tyler, aren't you the one who told me that when it comes to kids there's no such thing as 'or else' anymore?"

"That only applies to school, Lyme. Believe me."

They had a cop at the entrance to the gym to make sure nobody had alcohol on their breath or anything. I was afraid he'd frisk me and find my shaving cream. Lymie called me a jerk and pushed me through the door. The cop was so busy eyeing the older kids he didn't even seem to notice us.

Lymie made a beeline for the refreshment table. I stood around checking out the crowd. The kids were all restless, milling around under the bright lights waiting for something fun to happen. A few girls were dancing with each other like they always do. Every once in a while, somebody'd switch off the lights and this fat lady would tear across the floor and turn them back on. As soon as she got done, somebody'd turn them off from the other side, and she'd take off again. Not that it mattered. What with the hall lights and exit lights, you could still see fine, but it seemed like a pretty big deal to the fat lady.

There were about fifty parents standing around the sides gawking at everybody. And whenever somebody danced—a boy and a girl, that is—they'd all smile and poke one another like they thought it was the cutest thing in the world. It was all kind of depressing. I couldn't wait to get back outside.

"Come on, Ty. Let's go." Lymie stuffed a doughnut in my hand and pushed me toward the door. There were a couple of other kids with him. One was Jason Peters, a kid in my math class, and the other was Tommy Sheridan, who we all called Sher (pronounced like Cher) for short.

"Is this everybody?" I asked, hoping maybe Babette had chickened out.

"The rest of them'll meet us at the park," Lymie said.

When we left, all the parents gave us a dirty look. I was afraid to even look at the cop.

All Lymie's rotten ammunition was hidden under this bush in the park. He reached in and grabbed a paper bag out and started unloading it. The tomatoes were all individually wrapped in sandwich bags. The eggs were still in their cartons. Lymie's funny. He'll make a peanut butter sandwich and just stuff it in his pocket, but he'll individually wrap rotten tomatoes.

"Start putting tomatoes in your pockets," Lymie whispered. "Some of them are pretty gushy, so when we go to chuck 'em, we can just loosen the top of the bag and let 'em fly."

We all started stuffing them in. I put my shaving cream under the bush. I could get it later.

"We might as well leave the eggs in the cartons till we get there," Jason said.

"That's what I figured," Lymie said. "We'll divide them up later."

"HEY, YOU GUYS!"

The four of us almost jumped out of our skins. We turned and saw Toddie and Bart Phillips running toward us. God, everybody in four states must have heard them.

"Shut up, you guys!" Jason snarled. "You want us to get caught before we even get there?"

"Sorry," Bart said.

"Yeah," Toddie said.

I looked around. Still no sign of Babette. I was really hoping we'd be long gone before she showed up.

"Okay," Lymie said, talking real low. "We gotta make some final plans."

"Fine," I told him, "but make 'em quick."

Lymie started. "Babette said we should hit their house from the front and the back at the same time. That'll confuse 'em."

"Yeah, well Babette isn't here, so we can do what we want," I said.

"Yeah, who wants to get pinned down in their backyard?" Sher piped up.

"It won't be so bad," Jason said. "I know an easy way to get in there and get back out."

"I still want the front," Sher told us.

"Me and Ty'll take the back with Jason," Lymie said. When he saw me looking at him, he added, "Just think how good it'll feel Monday morning to tell Babette how we pelted Mr. Keepout. And from his backyard."

"Yeah," I said, "if we're *alive* Monday."

"Tyler, look," Lymie said, "I've been thinking about this. When the Keepouts hear things hitting their house, they're gonna run and investigate, right? And the chances are Mr. Keepout'll take the back because it's darker out there, and he's the guy. We get him with a couple of eggs and we're off like a shot."

"Do you have to say the word 'shot'?" I said. " 'Cause it wouldn't surprise me if he took one at us."

"Look, Ty." Lymie put his hand on my shoulder. "We'll be able to see him through the window. And if he's got a gun, we'll be a mile away before he gets out the door. What are you worried about? You're the fastest runner here."

"I'm not worried," I lied. "I just wanted to make sure you thought of everything."

"Let's do it," Jason said, and we all grabbed the last of the ammunition. When I turned around, I saw this huge shape rise up from behind another bush off to the side. My eyes bugged out. At first I thought it was some kid in a Bigfoot costume. It wasn't. It was Babette Flosdorf.

"I heard you try to weasel out," she said to me, "but you were too chicken to even chicken out."

I groaned.

To get to the Keepouts' backyard, we had to cut through a vacant lot on Maple and sneak up behind their old wooden fence. We hid there for a while, peering through the slats to make sure the coast was clear. It was hard to tell. The Keepouts had one of those big untended backyards filled with overgrown bushes and shrubs. The backyard was pitch dark and so was the house, which was spooky because I knew they were home. They'd never leave their house alone on Halloween. You could be sure of that.

"What do you think?" Lymie whispered in my ear.

"I don't know. They could be hiding behind one of those bushes."

"Buk, buk, buk!" That was Babette making chicken noises.

"They're probably not," Lymie said, "but keep your eyes peeled in case. We got . . ." He looked down at his watch.

78

"We got ten minutes before we hit 'em. If they're outside, we'll probably catch some movement by then."

We peered through the slats some more. My heart was beating like crazy. I couldn't wait to get it over with.

"With the lights out in the house, we'll never know if he's got a gun," I said.

"Buk, buk, buk!" Babette again.

"I just don't want anybody to get shot," I said. "I'm thinking about you, Babette. You're the biggest target."

"You little . . ."

"Shhhhh," Jason said. "They'll hear us. We're supposed to be a team, so quit fighting."

"Sorry, Babette," I said, but not like I meant it.

"You will be," Babette said.

"Seven minutes," Lymie said. "Let's get ready."

Lymie passed me some eggs. My jacket pockets were already full of tomatoes, and I knew if I put the eggs in my pants pockets, they'd get smushed the first time I crouched down. So I tucked in my shirt and stuck four of them in there. And boy, were they ever cold on my skin! I left one egg in each hand. I was armed and ready.

"Let's go," Lymie said. "We got less than four minutes to get close enough to open fire."

We all checked our watches, and one by one slipped through a broken part of the fence. Then we stood there waiting for somebody to make a move.

"Let's fan out so we'll be harder to catch," Jason told us.

"All right," Lymie said. "And when I give a yell, let everything ride."

Everybody fanned out. I was middle left and Babette was middle right. Lymie and Jason took the flanks. Pretty soon everybody had disappeared behind bushes and stuff. As soon as I was alone, I put my left-hand egg in my right hand, dropped to my knees, and crawled on my left hand. That way the eggs in my shirt hung down and stopped chilling my belly button. Every few seconds I'd freeze in mid-crawl and listen like a bird dog or an Indian or something. The grass was wet and cold enough to numb my hand. I could feel the dampness seeping through my pants to my knees. I crawled up behind a shrub and peeked around toward the house. I wasn't even close. I looked at my watch. Two minutes had passed. I'd have to pick up the pace or I wouldn't even get a shot in. I made kind of a frantic twenty-yard crawl and froze again, listening. Another crawl put me behind this humongous lilac bush on the edge of a clearing in front of the house. I set the eggs down and stood up, rubbing my hand and peeking around to see if I could spot the Keepouts peering out their windows. I couldn't. The windows might as well have been painted black. Only thirty seconds till attack time. I figured I'd wait until the last ten seconds, then rush into the clearing and fire away. If I was lucky, Mr. Keepout would poke his head out the door, I'd peg him a few times real quick, and be off like a streak. I picked up the eggs.

Twenty seconds . . . fifteen . . . I pulled my jacket around so it cradled the eggs in my shirt and took a deep breath. GERONIMO! I was off. As soon as I hit the clearing, I heard Lymie yell "Fire!" I slammed on my brakes, wung my arm back, and let an egg ride. Before it even splatted over the door, I switched hands and wung my arm back with the other egg. Something hit my finger tip and slithered down my arm and neck. The egg plunked down and broke on my shoulder. Next thing I knew something yanked me straight back off my feet and my butt slammed the ground. My left arm was pressed up against my head, and I felt this burning pain in my armpit and around my neck. It was like being in a nightmare. I panicked and flopped around on the ground like a fish out of water. More pressure on my neck and armpit and I felt myself being pulled backward some more. My wind was cut off. I couldn't breathe. *Oh God I'm dying*!

"Auuurrrgh!"

A light blasted my face and a huge foot pushed down on my chest. I gasped and flopped and tore at whatever was around my neck. It was a rope! *They got me! I'm dead. I'm being hung and I'm not even off the ground!*

Somebody yanked me to my feet and shoved me.

"I've got you now you little . . ." I didn't catch the last word. "Open the door, Elsie! I've got one!"

I squirmed and flailed and bit, but I couldn't get free. I felt cold metal on my temple and scrunched my head around as far as I could. A gun. *Oh God!* My legs went limp and I dropped to my knees. *Oh God don't shoot! Please don't shoot me!* Skidding on my knees, I saw the house getting closer. I still couldn't breathe right. I couldn't tell if the rope was blocking my wind or if my lungs were paralyzed with fear like my legs. My knees scraped up over two or three steps, and I was pulled inside. The door slammed behind me. Lights snapped on and somebody yanked me back into a chair. A hand holding a rope came around me and wrapped it around my chest and stomach twice. My left arm was still cranked up against the side of my head. I sat there looking like the Statue of Liberty on a break. Only I was crying something fierce and gasping for air in fits and starts.

I could feel hands working behind me, probably making a knot. I still hadn't seen any faces yet. Only hands. I heard a telephone being dialed. Then a woman's voice.

"We caught one. Maybe you'll believe us now." Pause. "Yes, this *is* she, and if you're not here in five minutes, we'll take care of him ourselves." She slammed the phone down. So hard it kind of rang.

I never thought I'd ever wish for the police so hard. I didn't care if I was in big trouble. I didn't care if they put me in a dirty damp cell and fed me bread and water. I didn't care if Mom grounded me for life and made me spend my free time doing extra homework. I just wanted to get out of there. Alive. To be able to breathe again. To go to school. Anything.

"Who are you?" Mr. Keepout said from behind.

When I sniffled instead of answering, he grabbed my hair and yanked my head back. I moaned.

81

"I said, 'Who are you?' "

"Tyler Mc . . . McAllis . . . ter," I gasped.

"Why do you come here? Why do you bother us?"

He moved around in front of me and let go of my hair. I stared up at him. He was kind of small and slinky-looking and he glared down at me with beady little rat eyes.

"Answer my husband!" Now Mrs. Keepout came around front. Her face was like a triangle: wide forehead, narrow chin. Her eyes bulged out so much she could watch me even when she turned away. Like one of Lymie's cows.

"I don't know," I said. My voice was shaking something wicked. My whole body was. "It's Halloween."

"Halloween? That's why you attack innocent people? Decent law-abiding citizens! Driving them from their homes!" She was facing the wall, but her bulgy left eye was still on me.

"No."

"No?" Mr. Keepout said. "You'd better have more to say than 'No'!" He bent down so close I could feel drops of spit on my forehead.

"No, sir," I squeaked.

"Don't you dare smart off to my husband!" She did an about-face and her other evil eye checked me out.

"No, ma'am."

She whirled around and locked both eyes on me.

"What right do you have . . . ?" She slinked toward me. "We paid for this home . . . It's ours . . . not yours . . . ours." She looked down at me like I was dirt, scum, vomit, and dog poop all rolled into one.

"My arm . . ." I said. "It hurts . . . and my neck."

"Listen to him, Elsie. Worried about nobody but himself. I oughta . . ."

I heard his heavy heels moving up behind me. I closed my eyes and squeezed out some more tears. I didn't want to know what he oughta.

Just then I heard a window smash and glass tinkling to the floor behind me. The heavy-heeled footsteps moved away. The door opened. Mr. Keepout shouted something.

I opened my eyes and cranked my head around as far as I could. No Keepouts. I struggled so hard to get free I nearly tipped over my chair. No use. I wasn't going anywhere.

I stopped struggling. I was aware for the first time of cold slime sliding off my stomach and around my sides. I could feel some of it seeping into my pants. The sickening sulfur smell of rotten eggs hit my nostrils. I thought I'd puke. They'd kill me if I did that. They'd think I did it on purpose.

I took as deep a breath as I could and looked around. The gun was on the kitchen table. Two big, shiny barrels staring me right in the eye. The door slammed again and a hand grabbed my hair and cranked my head back.

"Who are they?" Mr. Keepout boomed.

I was too terrified to even squeak. I squeezed my eyes shut.

"I said, *who are they?*"

"Kids!" I said, tears streaming. "Just kids like me."

"Let him go, Sam. Fun's over."

I opened my eyes and from where my head was cranked back, I could see an upside-down cop, gray uniform, gray cap, looking down at me. Another cop, a shorter guy, peeked out from behind him. I never even heard them come in.

Mr. Keepout let go of me, and my eyes followed the big cop as he came around front. He had a kind face, at least compared to the Keepouts.

"Are you all right, son?"

"They got a gun . . ." I gasped. "It was on my head . . . ! I . . ." I didn't know quite what I was saying. I just wanted the cops to get their gun.

The big cop pointed to the back of my chair and I could feel somebody fiddling with the rope, probably the little cop.

"Did you put a gun to his head?" the big cop said to the Keepouts. He seemed pretty mad.

"It was against my head!" I yelled. "Right up to my head!"

"Is that true?"

"Oh, for crying out loud," Mr. Keepout said, "it's loaded with blanks."

The big cop opened up the gun and popped the shells out. He looked at the Keepouts. "You know blanks can kill somebody at close range?"

"You cops," Mr. Keepout sneered. "Always worried about the criminals instead of protecting decent citizens."

"He's just a kid!" the big cop yelled. "A skinny little kid!"

"He's a criminal!" Mrs. Keepout yelled back at him. "A criminal! They come in all sizes. And if you don't book him, I'll call every newspaper in the country. You'll never work again."

The little cop finished unwrapping the rope. My arm flopped down like it was dead. I rotated my neck, trying to get the kinks out. The big cop felt around my shoulder and told me to pick up my arm to see if it still worked.

"You're lucky. It's not dislocated." I couldn't tell if he was talking to me or the Keepouts. He pushed my head back and looked at my neck. "Rope burns." He sounded disgusted. I did stink pretty bad.

"Come on, son." He helped me to my feet. "Let's get you out of this nuthouse."

"How dare you!" Mrs. Keepout said. "I'll report this to every newspaper in the country."

"Look, lady," the big cop said, and even though he wasn't yelling now you could hear the anger in his voice, "if you're lucky, I mean real lucky, this kid's parents won't sue you for every cent you've got and press criminal charges for reckless endangerment of a minor."

"Press charges on us!" she screamed. "You've got to be kidding!"

"He's a little kid, for Christ's sake," the big cop said. "A skinny damn little kid."

He pulled me toward the door and led me down the steps. At the bottom, he stopped and turned back to the open door.

"If you ever," he said slowly, "tie up a kid or point a gun at anybody again, I'll lock you up and throw away the key."

"The nerve!" Mrs. Keepout yelled. "You probably supply these kids with their drugs. That's why you're so anxious to protect them."

The door slammed and the cop led me around the side of the house to the street. Even if I was going to jail, I didn't care. Lymie and Jason and Babette and Toddie and Bart and Sher were all waiting by the cop car. Plus about thirty other kids. I leaned against the car with my head on the roof. I didn't want everybody to see me crying.

"Is he all right?" Lymie said.

"A little shaken up, that's all," the big cop said. "He'll be fine."

"I broke the window," Babette said. "The guy was getting ready to belt him, so I fired a rock through the window."

"Hmmph," the little cop said.

"Listen up," the big cop said, loud enough for everybody to hear. "As long as I have this many of you in one place, I want to tell you something." He waited till he made sure everybody was listening. "I don't want to ever hear that you kids are hanging around here or bothering these people again. Ever. This little guy . . ." He put his hand on my shoulder. "This little guy could have been hurt pretty bad tonight, and he's lucky he wasn't. You kids stay away from this place or somebody *will* get hurt, just as sure as you're standing here." He paused. "Do I make myself clear?"

Pretty much everybody mumbled that they understood. Except Babette. I heard her yell, "Scum!" and then I was pretty sure something splatted off the house. It was quiet for a second, everybody waiting to see if the cops would yell at her. They didn't. They probably knew better.

"I think it's time you kids headed home," the big cop told everybody. "You've had your fun." He opened the car door for me.

"Is he going to jail?" Lymie said.

"He's going home," the big cop said.

10

I missed the head-dredging ceremony in front of Badoglio's house on Saturday morning. I slept through it. Not that it would have mattered even if I got up. Mom wouldn't have let me out of the house anyway.

I couldn't really blame her. Mothers aren't usually too thrilled when their kid gets brought home by the cops. Especially when he's smeared inside and out with rotten eggs, and he's got rope burns around his neck and armpit from being dragged around by some maniac, and he's had a gun put up to his head. You should have seen it. She came flying out the door as soon as the cop car pulled up, and you could see her breathe this humongous sigh of relief when I got out in one piece. She hugged me, sulfur smell and all, for about five minutes—she was so happy I wasn't dead or something. Then she told me she was going to kill me.

Chuckie came running over from his cottage, and the big cop started in telling the whole story. The little bit I told while being hugged probably didn't make much sense. I was still shaking all over and I was afraid I'd start crying again. Chuckie pried Mom off me and sent me into the house to change my clothes and get cleaned up. When I got back downstairs, they were all in the kitchen having coffee. By then the cops had explained everything.

"You let me know what you want us to do about this, Ms. LaMar," the big cop said, and they both stood up to go. The big cop put his hand on my shoulder. "You'll be all right now, son.".

I looked at Mom and wasn't too sure.

For the next few hours I could barely stay awake, but I was afraid to go to bed. I knew for sure as soon as I got in bed and closed my eyes I'd start reliving the whole nightmare again. And even if I did fall asleep, I figured I'd end up tossing and turning and waking up in a cold sweat about fifty times. Plus I figured the more yelling I could get out of the way that night while I still looked pathetic, the better.

Mom had to go over every awful detail again and again, like she was writing a book or something. I might as well have let myself start crying in the first place and saved myself some effort. And to add to the confusion, Chuckie kept pacing around the kitchen table threatening to rip Mr. Keepout's face off. He'd've done it too, and Mom knew it. She had to keep interrupting her cross-examination of me to try and calm him down.

"I can't believe somebody'd do that to a little kid!" Chuckie said. He beat his fist into his palm and examined my neck for the tenth time. I was getting a lot of mileage out of that little kid stuff. From everybody but Mom.

"Chuckie, he's old enough to know better than to harass people." She glared at me. "Especially poor people who aren't quite right." She pointed to her head.

"He's a kid!" Chuckie said. "That's the kind of thing kids do on Halloween."

"This is one kid whose Halloween days are over. You can be sure of that." She paced around behind me. "I'm not saying what happened to him was right. My blood boils when I think about it. But I won't allow you to get into trouble because of this boy's thoughtlessness. When we cool down, we'll decide what should be done about those people. But if we do anything, we'll do it through the proper channels." Mom circled around in front of me. And started in again.

"If your friends told you to jump off a building, would you do it?"

Every mother I've ever known uses that one.

"If your friends told you to cut off your head, would you do it?"

That's one of Mom's own creations.

"Mom," I whined, slumping down in my chair. "Nobody told me to do anything."

"Oh, I see," Mom said. "You come up with these ideas yourself. Half the time you can't remember to tie your shoes, but you can think of these crazy ideas by the dozen."

It went on like that until I couldn't even hold up my head anymore. Not that that stopped Mom. She was so hyped up she kept lifting my head so she could say more stuff in my face. When I finally stumbled upstairs, I fell asleep on top of the covers without even getting undressed. In the morning I was all covered up. Mom probably yelled at me when she did that too, but I didn't hear her.

Mom didn't have much to say at breakfast (lunch for her), but at least she didn't seem as mad. She looked at me as I fiddled around with my cereal. I was too depressed to eat. I always get like that after something terrible happens to me. It's like a disaster hangover or something.

"I'm sorry," I said finally. I stared down at my bowl.

"I know," Mom said, taking a deep breath. "I am too." She paused. "Tyler, you'd have to be a mother to know how I felt last night."

"Not much chance of that," I said.

She smiled.

"It's funny," I said. "I never once in my life planned on getting in trouble. And I've been in trouble about a zillion times. I don't get it. Things just happen to me. I don't know . . . maybe I was born under a bad star or something."

That made her smile even more.

"I bet, Tyler, that if you really thought about it, you'd see that these things don't just happen. Like it didn't simply happen that you attacked that man's house. Or that you were in that river looking for those heads. These were decisions you made. Conscious decisions." She looked me over. "I only hope that this time you had a good enough scare so you learned your lesson once and for all."

"I did. Believe me, Mom, I'm not gonna be chucking eggs at anybody for about my next five lifetimes. I'm not gonna do anything. I mean it."

Mom smiled and shook her head. You could see she was wondering what stunt I might pull next.

The phone rang. It was Lymie, all excited.

"Tyler, they found our heads! You shoulda seen it. It was great!" And as kind of an afterthought. "Oh, yeah, are you all right?"

"Yeah," I said, "but I'm going to have to cool it for a while."

Mom gave me the evil eye.

"I'm going to have to cool it for good," I corrected.

Mom nodded.

"So tell me about . . ." I looked at Mom. "Tell me about this other thing you were telling me about. What did everybody say? Did they laugh or what?"

"No," Lymie said, all excited again. "That's what's so amazing! Those heads musta been so ugly they looked real. You shoulda seen it, Ty. Everybody was going crazy. You'd think they'd found gold or something."

"You're putting me on! No way."

"Yes way, Ty! I'm telling you the God's honest truth. And listen to this. When they took the heads away, they gave 'em a police escort! Can you believe it? For the same heads that Chuckie thought were so stupid-looking. Like they were afraid somebody might try to swipe 'em or something."

"Wow." I sat down. "Wow." I thought for a second. "Lymie, I'm not sure this is a good time for this."

"Relax, Ty. Nobody knows who made those things."

"Yeah, well what about Chuckie? What about my mother? What about Lester Phillips?"

All of a sudden I was aware of Mom standing about two feet in front of me. Staring down at my face.

"Christmas list, Mom." I tried to smile. "I mean, why wait till the last minute?"

"He's doing it again," Mom said, walking away. "He's not going to stop. Not until they put me away. Then maybe he'll . . ." Her voice faded out into the living room.

I couldn't believe it. Here I was with another major problem and my mother was running around talking to herself.

Our heads made the six o'clock news. And I was sitting right next to Mom. They showed these cops carrying them into the courthouse. I leaned in closer to get a better look. You couldn't see the heads very well, but I didn't need to. I knew they were ours.

"I recognize them," Mom said, leaning in closer too.

I took a hitching breath. "Huh?"

"Those are the police officers who brought you home last night."

I had the hiccups for like the next half hour.

11

The heads were going on display the following Saturday, the day of the big Badoglio celebration. It was supposed to be a tribute to Badoglio and kind of a fall field day all rolled into one. Where else but in Wakefield could you go to an art exhibit and then turn around and get into a sack race or a pie-eating contest or something? Ordinarily, I'd be all excited over an occasion like that. As it was, I was praying for rain.

My whole week was ruined. Whenever I heard the kids in school talking about the Badoglio heads, I'd sort of flinch and get this sinking feeling in my stomach. By Monday afternoon I saw my first Badoglio bumper sticker. It said "I'M PROUD TO BE FROM WAKEFIELD, BADOGLIO'S HOMETOWN." My knees almost buckled. Plus, everybody kept wanting me to tell them all about how I got dragged into the Keepouts' house and tied up. It was like seeing the Ghost of Trouble Past and knowing the Ghost of Trouble Future was on his way.

Mom knew something was up because when I get good and nervous I can't eat, but luckily it never dawned on her that the heads they'd dredged up were Lymie's and mine.

Mom's pretty smart about a lot of things, but her brain just doesn't work that way. It'd never even cross her mind that the two of us would deliberately do something that'd make the whole rest of the town want to kill us. What she did think was that I was still upset about the Keepout thing. Whenever she caught me looking worried, she'd give me a hug and say, "Don't dwell on it, hon. It's over and done with. Just think what a nice time we'll have at the Badoglio celebration." Then she'd stick food in front of me and I'd almost gag.

Chuckie caught on quicker. He cornered me in the garage on Wednesday as I was checking the air in my bike tires. He came slinking up to me wearing this big stupid grin.

"So, Ace," he said, "what's new?"

Since Chuckie wasn't one for idle chitchat, and he wasn't big on smiling either, I knew he had something on his mind.

"Not much, Chuckie. How about you?" I wasn't going to tell him any more than I had to.

"Same old stuff." He sat on the bumper of Mom's car and watched me fiddle around with the air pressure gauge. Both tires were fine, so I put the thing away.

"How's the neck coming along?" he said.

"It's all right." I came over and let him look at it.

"You were lucky," he said.

"I know," I said. "When that guy put that gun to my head, I thought I'd have a heart attack or something."

Chuckie shrugged. "That guy oughta be in jail." He paused. "I bet you learned your lesson though, huh?"

"Yeah." I looked at Chuckie. He had that same goofy grin back.

"I thought so." He punched my arm. "I bet it'll be a while before you land yourself in trouble again."

"Hope so." I went back to fiddling around with my bike.

"Hey, Ace, what do you think about those Badoglio heads they dredged up? Kind of exciting, huh?"

"I don't know." I pretended to check the tightness of my handlebars. "I'm not into art that much." I clamped my legs around my front wheel and cranked up and down on the handlebars.

"They're good and tight," Chuckie said. "They're not going anyplace."

"Sometimes they get loose from all the vibrations." I waited. Chuckie was still staring at me. "Maybe I'll oil the chain."

"Good idea." He watched me while I got the WD-40. "I thought maybe you and Lymie'd be interested in this Badoglio stuff. You know, having dabbled a little in art yourselves."

"That's right, Chuckie—dabbled. Past tense. We got laughed out of the business. Remember?" I sprayed the chain until oil was dripping all over the floor.

"Hey, don't drown the thing. Just coat it." He waited while I put the cap back on. "You know, I was thinking, Ace. Maybe I was a little hasty. I mean, what do I know about art? And I only saw those heads once. I've always heard that art is something you really have to develop a taste for. Like good wine. Or foreign films." He came over and put his hand on my shoulder. "Ace, I couldn't live with myself if I thought I'd discouraged two promising young artists with a hasty, ill-informed judgment."

Whenever Chuckie talked like that, I knew he was putting me on. "Don't worry about it, Chuckie," I told him. "Your judgment wasn't 'ill informed.' Me and Lymie aren't cut out to be artists anyway." I slid out from under his hand.

"How do you know? Maybe you are." He came slinking up to me again. "I'd feel better if . . . I don't know . . . if I at least took another look at those heads and really gave them a fair chance." He was smiling the way foxes always smile in cartoons.

"Forget it, Chuckie. We don't even want to be artists. Really."

"Still, I'd feel a whole lot better if I could see those things again. What if you had all this potential and I . . ."

He groped the air with his hands. "Where are they anyway, Ace?"

"I don't know. They're around someplace." I suddenly felt the need to adjust my seat.

"Come on, Ace. Get 'em out. I promise I won't laugh this time."

I stopped fiddling with my seat and looked up. Chuckie was wearing that cartoon fox smile again.

"All right, Chuckie. If you got something to say, say it."

"What do you mean?" Chuckie said, making his eyes big and trying to act real innocent. He gave this humongous shrug and sat on a sawhorse.

"You know what I mean. You come in here all hyped up over those stupid heads. I know what you're thinking." I walked over to where Chuckie was sitting, bent down, and poked my face in front of his face. "Two stupid-looking heads turn up in the river. And two stupid-looking heads turn up missing from our garage." I jabbed my finger into his chest. "And don't tell me you didn't look already."

"You know, Ace, now that you mention it, I am having the littlest bit of trouble explaining that coincidence. If I didn't know better . . ." He studied my face.

I went over and sat next to him on the sawhorse.

"Chuckie?"

"Yeah, Ace?"

"Whaddaya think I should do?"

"About what?"

"Chuckie, cut the crap, will ya? You know what I'm talking about. Mom's gonna really kill me this time. That is unless some crazy townsperson guns me down first."

"Aren't you exaggerating a little?"

"I hope so, but maybe not. Chuckie, this is big news around here. They brought in a TV crew for crying out loud! Everybody's talking about those heads. You know, how they're putting Wakefield on the map and everything. Those people aren't gonna be too thrilled when they find out me and Lymie made those heads with a moto-tool and a Black and Decker drill set."

94

"No! You're kidding me!" Chuckie wrapped his fingers around his jaw and tried to look all amazed. "Those heads are *yours*? I had no idea!"

"Cut it out, Chuckie. I'm serious."

Chuckie looked at me and smiled. Not that goofy grin he had before, just a regular smile.

"It's also pretty funny, Ace. You gotta admit."

"Yeah, well you're not the one who's gonna get in trouble."

I stared at the floor feeling miserable. Chuckie put his hand on my shoulder again.

"Look, Ace. It might not be so bad. Listen. There's two art critics coming in tomorrow night, and they're gonna spend all day Friday studying those heads, right?"

I nodded.

"Okay. Only they won't have to study them all day before they realize they're as phony as a couple of three-dollar bills. The whole thing'll probably take about two minutes. No big deal. They'll make their announcement and that'll be that. Nobody'll grab a rope and round up a posse or anything. Wakefield will have had its thrill and gotten a little publicity. They'll still hold the Badoglio day and everybody'll have a good time, and the whole thing will fizzle out."

I looked at Chuckie. I felt this little glimmer of hope. "You think so?"

"Yeah, I do. How many people know about you guys making those heads anyway?"

"Only you . . . and me and Lymie, of course . . . and Lester Phillips, but he's only a little kid . . . and . . . oh, no . . ." My stomach sank again. I groaned. "And Mom. And when she finds out the heads they found are phonies it's only a matter of time before she puts two and two together."

"So?"

"What do you mean 'so'? I promised her I wouldn't do any more stupid things. This'll be it, Chuckie. I'm telling you, she's gonna go nuts on me. I know it."

"Look, Ace, what's she gonna do—throw you out on the street? Beat you till you're black and blue? She worries about you, that's all. But this head thing is different. You can't drown making a phony head. Or catch pneumonia. Or get tied up by some crazy lunatic and his wife. See, Ace, she worries when you do things that are dangerous. Who knows? She might even find this amusing."

I looked at Chuckie. "You think so?"

Chuckie thought. "No," he said and stood up. "Now that I think about it, she'll probably kill you."

I stood up. "Chuckie, why do you do stuff like this to me? Aren't I a likeable kid? Basically? Do I deserve this or something?"

"I'm sorry, Ace. Maybe I shouldn't tease you so much. Yeah, you're a likeable kid. And I don't even like kids. But you gotta admit, you do get into some funny situations."

"But this isn't funny, Chuckie. Not to me."

"Ace, what are you so worried about? What's the worst thing that can happen to you?"

I thought. "I could get grounded."

"Right, and you're already grounded."

"I could lose my allowance."

"What do you need money for? You're a *kid*. You have nice clothes. You get fed every day. What else do you need?"

"We'll probably both have to sit through another one of those family discussions."

All of a sudden Chuckie clutched his chest and fell against the workbench. "A family discussion! No, please. Anything but that. Beat me! Shoot me! Torture me! But not another family discussion!" He stumbled toward the door, bashing into things like a drunk. "I gotta get outta town. I can't take this anymore. I gotta . . ." He stumbled outside. The door closed behind him. I walked over to the window and I could see Chuckie stumbling across the yard, still talking to himself. Once he even fell down and started flopping around on the ground. In the past two months, Chuckie had gotten to be such a nut. I mean, he didn't

96

even know if I was still watching him or anything.

I'd've laughed if a car saw him, slammed on its brakes, and the people came running, thinking he was having a heart attack or something. I'd've laughed my head off.

12

Mrs. Estelle Hildegarde was the person in Wakefield who was kind of unofficially in charge of art and literature and stuff like that. Her husband had been a doctor, but years ago he'd been killed in a car accident. After that, she didn't have anything to do but read books and look at pictures and go to plays and concerts—that kind of thing. But not movies. She didn't believe in them. And she didn't even own a TV, a fact she'd slip into every conversation she could. And to get people out from in front of *their* TVs, she was always organizing poetry readings and art exhibits and historical lectures at the library.

So this whole Badoglio thing was right up her alley. She was the one who contacted the two big Badoglio experts in New York and made arrangements for them to come to Wakefield to study our heads.

On Thursday night a couple hundred people, including Lymie and me, were waiting around in front of Mrs. Hildegarde's house for the critics to arrive. It turned out I wasn't grounded half as bad as I was supposed to be because Mom decided I needed to get my mind off what happened at the Keepouts'. Mrs. Hildegarde and the mayor and the whole town council had gone to the Albany County Airport to pick up the critics. They took four cars to pick up two guys, which nobody found too strange except Lymie and me. A bunch of people gave Lymie a dirty look when he said, "What are they gonna do, put half a guy in each car?" I cringed. It just went to show that to these people this art stuff was no laughing matter.

Pretty soon somebody yelled, "Here they come!" and you could feel the excitement kind of ripple through the crowd. I looked down Main Street and saw two Lincoln Town Cars and the mayor's Cadillac, followed by Mrs. Hildegarde's 1965 Imperial—original paint job, not a speck of rust on it. They were cruising slowly toward us like a presidential motorcade or something. I poked Lymie and we ran up under the carport. Everybody gawked as the four cars pulled into the circular driveway. The first three drove right through the carport, but Mrs. Hildegarde stopped her car right next to us. Two guys we didn't know were in the back seat. They just sat there staring straight ahead like they didn't even realize they'd already gotten to where it was they were going. Lymie bent over and stuck his nose up to the glass and studied them as if they were in a Sea World exhibit or something. I stepped up and popped the door open before the whole crowd could stick its face up to the window. I probably opened it a little harder than I had to so I could crunch the glass into Lymie's nose and teach him some manners. Then, so he could really see how civilized people act, I popped Mrs. Hildegarde's door open and even offered her my arm.

She looked up at me and smiled. "My, what a considerate young man!"

I'd never helped a lady out of a car before, so I didn't know if I was supposed to pull on her arm or just let her pull on mine. I let her start pulling and then I kind of helped her along. It got her out anyway.

"Thank you, young man," she said as I closed the door. "You are a credit to young people everywhere."

I heard Lymie snort behind me, but I didn't care. I felt pretty good.

By now we were surrounded by all the guys who got out of the other three cars, not to mention the rest of the crowd, which was closing in fast. The council guys and the mayor immediately tried to shield the critics from everybody else. You could tell they didn't want to share them.

The first critic to get out was a fat guy in a gray wool suit that was wrinkled pretty bad from travelling, and would have been wrinkled worse except he was too fat for it. His sport coat stretched around the small of his back, over his butt, and around his gut. The button holding it closed would probably have killed somebody if it ever let loose. He tossed his head back and looked over the crowd like some rancher looking over his herd. Then he started brushing himself off with his hands. The mayor and the council guys looked like they were trying to decide if they should be helping brush him off. They didn't, but one of them patted the fat guy's elbow.

Then the second critic got out. He was skinny and his suit fit him, but he looked pretty out of it too. He wore these black horn-rimmed glasses and his face reminded me of this turtle I used to have. Plus, he kept scrunching his face up like he had a fly on his nose he was trying to shake off. And he kept his hands behind his back all the time, even when he climbed out of the car. It looked like he was handcuffed or something.

Both guys got whisked into Mrs. Hildegarde's house before we could study them too much more.

"Well?" I said to Lymie. "What do you think?"

"They look like the kind of guys that'd like somebody like Badoglio."

"I don't care how goofy they look," I told him. "I just want this whole thing to blow over as soon as possible. Come on. Let's get out of here."

"Certainly, Tyler, my good man. May I offer you my arm?"

"No, but I'll offer you mine," I said and punched him.

"Now, now," Lymie said and got me in a headlock. "Raising your fists in anger? That's hardly being a credit to young people everywhere, now is it?"

All day Friday I waited. On pins and needles. I figured as soon as those critics discovered how phony the heads were, we'd hear about it at school. Nothing ever happened in town that didn't get spread around the whole school before one period had passed. I was getting more and more antsy as the day went on. By lunch I was going crazy.

"I don't like it, Lymie," I said. "What if they're really mad and they're dusting those heads for prints or something?"

"Naaah," Lymie said. "Too many people had their hands on those things Saturday. Probably they're just trying to figure out the best way to break the bad news to the public. They're probably afraid a riot will break out or something."

"Don't say things like that, Lymie. Not even joking around."

"Are you gonna eat that pizza?" Lymie asked, poking his head over my tray.

"I think I'm getting an ulcer."

"Then you're not going to eat it?"

"Take it, Lymie!" I picked it up and waved it in his face. "If that's all you care about, just take it!"

"Thanks." Lymie grabbed the pizza out of my hand and stuffed half of it in his mouth. "I'm telling you, Ty, just keep your mouth shut and nobody's gonna get in any trouble." He stuffed the rest of the pizza in his mouth. "Plus you really should eat. You look kinda peaked."

After school, I waited on the front steps for Mary Grace to come out. Lymie'd kill me if he knew, but I really needed to talk to somebody about the heads. Somebody whose philosophy consisted of more than "Keep your mouth shut." And somebody who wouldn't think it was funny like Chuckie did. And somebody who was concerned, but who wouldn't go nuts on me like Mom would. Somebody like Mary Grace.

I sat on the center rail and looked out over the sea of heads. A couple times I almost got knocked off by bigger kids who were fooling around and not watching where they were going. On Friday afternoon you can get trampled if you don't watch it. I gripped the railing tighter.

"If you're waiting for Mary Grace, you can forget it, McAllister."

I cranked my head around. It was Babette Flosdorf.

"Why?" I said.

"'Cause she's staying after, that's why." She started to go.

"What for?"

"For French club, ya nose."

"Babette . . . ?"

Babette stopped and looked up at me. I couldn't think what to say.

"What?" she snapped and glared at me with her fists clenched. You could tell she was afraid I was going to blow out my cheeks or make some kind of a fat joke. I wondered why I never noticed that before, how she was kind of afraid of what people might do to her.

"I don't have all day, buttface." She took a step toward me.

"How come you stuck up for me?" I blurted out. "You know, when you thought Mr. Keepout was gonna belt me, and you threw that rock to stop him?"

Babette folded her arms and looked me over. "I don't like that guy," she said. "He's mean. And I don't like people picking on people who are smaller than them."

"Thanks," I said. "I know we haven't been . . . I don't know, like best friends or anything . . ."

"Don't sweat it. And don't take it personally. I slammed a guy in the face once for teasing a dog."

"Still it was pretty nice . . ." I said.

"Yeah, yeah, save it," she said. She turned and started down the steps again. I sat there watching her. And I felt

102

kind of sorry. If she didn't have Mary Grace, she probably wouldn't have one friend in the whole world. She'd always kind of barge in on other kids' groups like she did with us when we raided the Keepouts, but she didn't have a group of her own. I hate it when I think about people being alone. Maybe because I've been a new kid so many times.

I hopped off the railing and took off down the steps. "Hey, Babette, wait up!" I yelled.

She stopped and gave me the eye.

"Where ya going?" I said. "You going home or what?"

"What's it to ya?" She started walking again.

I got in front of her and walked backwards. I always end up talking to people that way. One of these days I'll probably back off a cliff or something.

"Look, Babette," I told her. "I'm going down to town hall to see if anybody knows anything about those Badoglio heads. Wanna come?"

"What do I care about those stupid things?"

"I don't know. It's art. Besides, it's something to do. Come on."

"I'll have to see if I can clear my social calendar," she said.

Then she laughed and punched me in the arm. Hard. I almost went flying.

About twenty people were hanging around in front of the town hall. Most of them looked pretty bored. They reminded me of the people I used to see hanging around the movie sets where Mom and Chris were working, killing a whole day just trying to catch a glimpse of a star or something. Babette and I wandered around listening to see if anybody knew anything. Which as far as we could tell, nobody did.

"Maybe we should ask somebody," I said.

"Why are you so spazzed out about those stupid heads?" Babette said. "I can't believe it. You're as bad as all the other people in this stupid town." She pointed to a guy standing in front of us wearing a green plastic jacket that said "I'M PROUD TO BE FROM WAKEFIELD, BADOGLIO'S HOMETOWN." The lady standing next to him was wearing this blue plastic jacket that said "I'M PROUD TO BE A FARMWIFE." They both turned around and glared at Babette. Babette glared back at them. "If they were really proud, they wouldn't need to advertise it. What a joke!"

By now some of the other people were giving us the eye. And a lot of them were wearing pins and T-shirts and jackets and stuff—all saying how proud they were about Badoglio and everything. Babette stuck her tongue out at the crowd. At the whole crowd! I wanted to crawl into a hole and disappear.

"You got that right, honey."

I turned around. Buster Rudzinski, all three or four hundred pounds of him, was standing there chuckling. Buster owned a game room on lower Main Street and spent most of his working day cooking greasy food for anybody crazy enough to order it and yelling at kids who even looked at his games wrong. He chewed on his big cigar and shook his head.

"Yeah," he said, "they're a pretty sorry-looking bunch, ain't they?" He waved his hand out toward the crowd.

"Hey, Buster," I said, "I didn't know you liked art." Buster was the last guy in town I'd expect to be into something like that.

"Art your butt, McAllister. If I liked art, which I don't, I wouldn't be hanging around here." He chomped down on his cigar and chuckled through his teeth.

"Say, Buster," I said, and tried not to sound too anxious, "did you hear any news? You know, about the heads?"

"Like what?"

"Like are they *real*?" I almost squeaked.

"Oh, they're real enough," Buster said, smirking. "I seen 'em myself, solid rock with faces on the front. If you could call what they're wearing faces." He rocked back on his heels and guffawed.

"You know what I mean, Buster," I said. "Did they find out whether those things were chiseled by Badoglio?"

104

"He wants to know if they're valuable or just overgrown paperweights," Babette said.

Buster looked down at me. He was scowling now. "I thought you were smart, McAllister. At least smarter than these yo-yos." He jabbed his thumb toward town hall. "Suppose these two guys who call themselves experts come tearing out here and tell us that Badoglio really did chisel those heads. Big deal. Ain't they the exact same heads they'd be even if they found out they'd been chiseled by some scrawny little clod like you?"

A shiver shot up my spine when he said that. I think I even flinched.

"Think about it, McAllister. No matter what those pantywaists in there decide, we're talking about the same exact heads, ain't we?" He looked at me. "Well, ain't we?"

The lady with the blue "I'M PROUD TO BE A FARMWIFE" jacket turned around and said, "If I knew as little as you did, I don't think I'd open my mouth and let everybody know."

Buster looked at the lady, long and hard, like she was a piece of dog poop he'd just stepped in or something. Finally he said, "You wouldn't need to. You'd probably be wearing a jacket that said 'I'M PROUD TO BE STUPID.' "

Chuckie pulled into the driveway at eleven o'clock that night. I'd been waiting at my bedroom window for him for about two hours.

"Hey, Chuckie!" I whisper-yelled out the window. "Any news about the heads?"

"They're not saying a word, Ace."

I didn't know if he meant the critics or the heads. Knowing Chuckie, he probably meant the heads.

I went to bed. I was almost too tired to worry about it anymore. Almost.

13

By Saturday morning I was in a wicked sweat. All night long I'd tossed and turned, and whenever I drifted off I'd see those stone faces leering at me. Only the faces kept changing. First they'd be the things we chiseled. Then they'd be the mayor and some council guy. Then Mrs. Hildegarde. Then the two critics. Then Mom. They'd appear over and over again in different combinations. And they'd all be leering and pointing at me. Only I don't remember how because they didn't have hands.

The phone rang next to my bed, and I must have popped a good foot up in the air. Mom yelled that it was for me. I picked it up, but I was so out of it I couldn't remember what to say.

"Hey, scumbag! You there?"

Lymie. I didn't say anything. I just stared at the phone.

"Look, I know how you are when you first wake up, but this is important. Slap yourself a few times or something."

"Slap . . . you . . ." I mumbled. I looked at the clock. It was already nine.

"Good, Ty, you're speaking. Why don't you just slap yourself and *pretend* it's me."

"Shuddup . . ."

"If *I* shut up, it wouldn't be much of a conversation, would it?"

"Whaddaya want?"

"News," he said. "What's the scoop on the heads?"

I yawned. "Nothing."

"What do you mean, nothing? Today's the big day."

"I can't help it," I said. "There's no news."

"Did you go out last night? They might have announced it then."

"No, but they didn't. Chuckie was out till eleven and he'd've heard."

"That's not good."

"No kidding, Lyme. This whole thing isn't good. That's what I've been trying to tell you all week."

"They're probably gonna announce it right at the park."

I groaned. "Oh, God. We're dead."

Lymie thought for a minute. "Ty, I still say we'll be all right if we just keep our mouths shut."

"Now that's original advice."

"Look, I can tell you're in one of those moods. Just cool out. I'll be coming in around noon. We'll talk then."

I hung up the phone. Then I flopped back on my bed and groaned again.

"I think I'm sick."

"You think you're sick? On a Saturday? That's a new one." Mom sat on the edge of my bed and felt my head. "You don't have a fever." She looked down my throat. "Your throat's fine. What exactly do you feel like?"

"Sick," I said.

"Tyler, you've been moping around like this ever since those awful people scared you last week. Look at you. You're as white as a ghost." She smoothed my hair back. "Would it help to talk about it?"

"Mom, we talked about it almost all night last Friday. I'd just as soon forget about it."

"You're right, hon. You're absolutely right. We'll get

your mind off it. We'll go to the park today and look at the exhibits and play games and eat whatever we want. We'll have ourselves a great time. Come on, admit it. Aren't you a little excited about those Badoglio heads?"

I almost choked. "Maybe excitement is bad for me," I said. "What if I have something like mono where you need lots of rest?"

Mom shook her head. "I already thought of that. But you don't have swollen glands. And you don't have a sore throat. Besides, I know you pretty well, and this is the way you always act when you're upset about something. You just need to get out and have a little fun, experience a little of life's gusto." She got me in a headlock and gave me a noogie. "What do you say, tough guy?"

"Yeah," I said and tried to smile.

"Chuckie!" I yelled. "Come on! This is important!"

Chuckie had been sucking up leaves with the little John Deere tractor, but when he saw me coming toward him, he turned off the leaf thing, shifted into high gear, and made me chase him around in circles. Finally I stopped and just stood there. Chuckie did a few more loops and then drove up to me.

"Did you want me, Ace?" he said, innocent as can be.

I rolled my eyes and pulled the throttle down. "Chuckie, you gotta go with me to the park today."

He poked me in the ribs. "Why, Ace? You got a couple of women lined up for us?"

"Quit clowning around," I said. "I'm serious."

Chuckie flicked the key off and swung his leg over to the side. "Speak," he said.

"Are you gonna make fun of me?"

Chuckie stared at me for a second. "I was only trying to get you to lighten up, Ace. But you're really upset, aren't you?"

I nodded and looked away. I was afraid I might start to cry. "Promise you won't laugh at me?"

"I promise." He got off the seat, picked me up by the

108

elbows, and set me on it. Just like I was a feather or something. "Okay, Ace, I'm listening."

I looked at him. "I think I'm going crazy." I leaned forward and studied his face. "Don't laugh," I warned him.

"I'm not," he said. "Go on."

"That's all there is. I think I'm going crazy."

"Ace, you're not going crazy."

"How do you know I'm not? Are you a psychiatrist or something? Look, Chuckie, I read a lot, you know. You're not talking to Lymie or somebody, where you can just tell him something and he'll believe it."

"Ace, I'm telling you . . ."

"Chuckie, I've got all the symptoms of a severe clinical depression." I counted on my fingers. "Number one: I'm depressed. Number two: My appetite's gone and I'm losing weight. Number three: I can't sleep at night. Number four: When I do get to sleep, I have these crazy nightmares. And number five: I'm a nervous wreck, and I have this constant sense of doom. You know, like paranoia. Like I know something terrible's gonna happen." All while I was talking, I watched Chuckie like a hawk to make sure he didn't laugh or anything. He didn't. But when I got done, he shook his head.

"This is all about the heads, isn't it? And the art exhibition. You're really scared about this, aren't you?"

I nodded. "That's what I've been trying to tell you. And you think it's so funny." I slumped back in the seat. "Chuckie, this has been a bad week. Last Friday I got attacked by some lunatic family. I could've been killed or something. And all this week I've been a nervous wreck because practically the entire town is wearing these T-shirts saying how proud they are about this Badoglio stuff. Only the two things they're most proud of are phonies, and today they're gonna find out. And they're gonna want blood. I'm telling you, this is no joke!"

Chuckie put his hand on my shoulder. "I'm sorry, Ace. I didn't know how much this was getting to you. I should've realized, considering what you've been through." He sat on

109

the grass and looked up at me. "But you're not going crazy, and you're not clinically depressed or anything like that. It's just like you said. You've had a bad week, that's all."

I got down off the tractor and sat next to him.

"Chuckie?"

"Yeah, Ace?"

"Are you gonna go? You know . . . to the park?"

"Don't worry, I'll be there. But I still think you're worried over nothing." He leaned back on his elbows. "Look. Early this morning they brought in the Badoglio exhibit. You know, a bunch of his paintings and some of the real heads he made. And you wanna know what I think they're gonna do?"

I nodded.

"They're gonna take all the heads, the real ones and the fake ones, and set them out side by side so everybody can see how they're different. They'll have these cards or something printed up explaining the different features you look for when you study that kind of thing. And they'll show how they can tell that the two new heads are fakes. That way instead of everybody getting mad, they'll feel like they're getting more intelligent, like they have the inside scoop on something. They'll be able to explain to all their out-of-town relatives how they knew all along why the heads weren't genuine."

"You think so?" I leaned back on my elbows. "You don't think they're gonna come looking for the guys who did the phonies?"

"Ace, those phony heads could've been there for years. Who's to say? Badoglio might've been trying to teach some art student how to be a sculptor. And when the guy made those things, Badoglio might've gotten so upset that he threw both the student *and* the rocks out."

He looked to see if that got a smile out of me. It did.

"Wow," I said, and then I thought for a minute. "So my only real problem is going to be with Mom. When she goes through the exhibit and sees the head I made sitting there . . ."

"Big deal," Chuckie said. "I'm not blind. I see the way you handle your mother. You'll look at her in that certain way, like some kind of sick puppy . . . and even when she's yelling at you, you know she's already starting to melt and you're going to get off pretty much scot-free. And don't tell me that's not true."

I gave him a jab to the ribs. "You think I'm a little faker?"

Chuckie laughed. "Only some of the time. But even when you're genuinely upset, you get that same sad puppy face."

"You make me sound like Reginald."

"Hey, Ace, if the flea collar fits . . ."

I laughed.

Chuckie sat up. "So you feel better now? I mean, no more nervous breakdowns or anything?" He messed up my hair.

"Yeah, I do. Thanks."

"And, Ace . . ."

"Yeah, Chuckie?"

"I know it's easier said than done, but try and forget about the Keepouts. You know, they're probably more scared of you than you are of them. That's why they act the way they do."

I thought about that. "Yeah," I lied, "probably." But I knew they couldn't possibly be more scared of me than I was of them.

14

Mom and I went on to the park ahead of Chuckie. Which I figured was just as well. I'd thought about what he'd said, and I was pretty sure he was right about Mom being the only one I'd really have to deal with when it all came out about the heads and when she realized one of them had been sleeping in my bed. And since Chuckie was on to my puppy-face look, I'd feel funny having to do it in front of him. And if I was too self-conscious, it might not even work, and I'd end up getting grounded for the rest of the year. Besides, Chuckie said he'd be there in plenty of time for all the speeches and ceremonies and everything. Just in case.

It was still pretty quiet at the park when we got there. Mom wanted plenty of time to browse around and look at all the artwork before the big crowds arrived. Which was fine with me. The less people around when Mom saw my head, the better.

Most of the people there were busy setting up tables and booths and stuff. I stopped for a while and watched a bunch of guys filling up the "Dunk a Fireman" tank with a big hose from the fire truck. The guy you were supposed to dunk was already pacing around in his black rubber suit which he probably hoped would keep him from catching pneumonia. He stuck a finger in the water and one of the other guys yelled, "Cold enough for ya, Bob?" and gave a big toothless laugh. After a few minutes, Mom tugged on my arm and we moved on.

Pretty soon Mom ran across some lady she knew, one of Mrs. Oster's friends, and they started talking about Badoglio. I knew if I tugged on *her* arm I'd get yelled at, so I wandered over and started helping some lady move goldfish from a huge tank into little fish bowls so people could win them by shooting Ping-Pong balls at them. Mom came up behind me just as I caught the last fish. The lady told me thanks and said that if there were any fish left at the end of the day, she'd give me a free one. Mom said, "Oh, how nice," but I noticed she didn't say I could have one. Probably part of her "You have yet to show me you're responsible enough to have another pet" policy. And all because I'd lost my turtle in the backyard when I was seven.

Every once in a while it dawns on me what a slave you are when you're a kid.

The Badoglio exhibit was in a trailer that'd been dragged up from New York City. You had to climb up the steps and file past all Badoglio's stuff, which was behind this velour rope, until you got to the exit. It was the same kind of setup that traveling carnivals used to display a bearded lady or a two-headed dog or something. Except this was free, which was like they were admitting right off the bat that there wasn't anything in there worth paying to see.

For the first ten feet or so there weren't any exhibits, so we had to stand around in line behind a bunch of people who were already in there looking everything over. Most of them were pretty old. Old people always seem to show up about ten hours early for everything. I mean, if you go out for breakfast, you'll see old people having lunch, and if you go out for lunch, they'll be having dinner. That seems to be the way people get when they get old although I can't imagine myself ever getting old enough so *I'd* be early for everything.

Even though we were surrounded by people, Mom decided to start a conversation. "Honey, you look so much better than you did this morning." I felt her arm creeping up around my shoulder. "I knew it'd do you a world of good to get out." She kissed me.

"Mom," I said through my teeth as quiet as I could, "we're in *public*." I looked around to see if anybody had seen her touch me. People on both sides were watching us like we were a TV show or something. Most of them had probably seen Mom on TV lots of times, so maybe they thought we were.

Mom smiled. "Oh, whatsamatter?" she said in baby talk. "Don't you like your old mother anymore?" Then she reached out and pinched my cheeks.

I yanked my face loose. "Yeah, I like you," I said, hoping nobody heard me, "but I'm in the eighth grade."

Mom laughed. "Oh, come on. You're not that old. Indulge me a little." She tweaked my nose.

Then the lady behind us got into the act. "That's just like my grandson, Tommy. He used to love to cuddle up with me while I'd read him a book. Every night he'd look forward to that. Cuddling up with Grandma. Now he's in tenth grade and I can't touch him with a ten-foot pole."

"I know," Mom said. "I should be used to this by now. My older son went through that same phase. They grow up so fast, don't they?"

Then the old lady in front piped up. "It's always the same. You slave over them all the time they're growing up—changing their diapers, feeding them and what not—and then they get to that age where they don't even want to be seen with you. I raised five of them. I oughta know."

The old guy with her looked at me and shook his head.

Mom smiled. "They want to be independent. I guess we can't change that."

Next thing you knew they'd all introduced themselves, all the ladies that is, and they started telling each other everything they could think of about their children and grandchildren and nieces and nephews and even their dogs and cats. I just stood there. I've been standing in lines my whole life and I've never said "boo" to anybody, but Mom can't stand in line for two minutes without learning everybody around her's life history and then telling ours. I can't believe it. She still gets Christmas cards from people she met in line at the Department of Motor Vehicles.

Luckily the line started moving before they got out baby pictures or anything, and we got up to where the Badoglio stuff was. First there were a couple of oil paintings. One I recognized right off the bat. It was the picture of the guy playing the violin that I'd seen in the modern art book. The other was a portrait of some artist who was a friend of Badoglio's when he lived in Paris for a while. Neither picture was that great. The painting of the violin guy was even more smeary-looking when you saw it full-sized right in front of you. And the portrait of the artist reminded me a little of Alfred E. Neuman, the guy who's always on the cover of *Mad* magazine. Only this guy had a humongous long neck and one of his eyes was higher than the other. And it wasn't just like he was cocking an eyebrow or something—the whole eye was higher. Mom was busy telling me about things like elongation of features and Greek purity of form, but I didn't get most of it. Even if I didn't have most of my mind on trying to get a peek down the line to see if my head was about to turn up, that kind of talk just wasn't as much fun when Lymie wasn't around.

"Mom," I said finally, "face it. The guy couldn't paint."

Which was a mistake to say when I should have been busy buttering her up. Mom has this way of speaking with her eyes when she's in a crowd, and her eyes started saying something pretty nasty to me. But her voice said, "We're a little close to them, that's all, hon. They need to be viewed from a distance in order to be appreciated."

"Yeah. Maybe you're right," I said, trying to be nice for once. "Too bad the trailer wasn't bigger so we could get further away."

Her eyes spoke to me again. She thought I was still being wise.

I thought about trying to explain that I was trying to agree with her, but I decided maybe I should quit while I was ahead. I could hear other people trying to come up with intelligent things to say. The lady ahead of us who'd raised the five kids said to the old guy, "He really believed in using long, firm brush strokes, didn't he, George?" And George said, "I wouldn't've let him paint my barn." The lady got all embarrassed and turned to Mom and said, "George is always joking," and George said, "no I ain't." The lady kept smiling, but I could see her dig her fingers into his arm.

I peeked ahead again to see if I could see my head yet. I couldn't. Even with all the things Chuckie had said to calm me down, I could feel myself getting more nervous by the minute. And when I get nervous, I usually get a little hyper. Before I even knew it I started drumming my fingers on the silver post in front of me, and every few seconds I'd pretend to whack Mom on the head and make a cymbal sound. Mom gave me the same kind of arm gouge that George got.

I leaned back as far as I could and checked for my head again. Finally, when the lady ahead of us stepped forward I could see a bunch of wooden boxes lined up side by side about fifteen feet away. I felt a chill go up my spine. I had a pretty good idea the stone sculptures would be in those boxes, but I couldn't see into them yet. I looked further ahead and all of a sudden my eyes bugged out. About twenty feet away was a nude. A *real* nude—not like the ones Lymie'd found in the modern art book. Except for having a long nose and hairy pits, this one wasn't bad. George must've spotted her too. I heard his wife say, "Put your eyes back in your head, you old fool."

The line seemed to start moving faster. Maybe people were embarrassed to stand in front of the nude, or maybe George was pushing, but before I knew it we were right in front of the boxes. When I looked back from my third or fourth peek at the nude, there they were—these stone heads—staring back at us. There were three boxes and three heads, and they all looked pretty much the same as the one we'd seen in the book, with long horse faces and big noses. I gave this little sigh of relief. As far as I could tell, there were no more boxes, which probably meant our heads weren't even there.

I edged on. I was already thinking about how I should go past the nude—whether I should keep my head down and kind of act like I didn't see it, or whether I should act cool and look at it like I would've any of the other pictures. But that might be embarrassing with those ladies on both sides of me. Not to mention my own mother right next to me. I hoped she didn't start explaining to me in front of everybody how armpit hair was considered very beautiful in Badoglio's day.

Just when I was in the middle of thinking about all that, I happened to look down in front of me. And there it was. Lymie's head. It wasn't in a box. It was lying flat on the counter, probably because it didn't have any neck or pedestal or anything like the real Badoglio heads. It still looked like it had just been gonged over the head with a frying pan or something, and it still looked like it was thinking about throwing up. I was too.

Right next to it was the head I made. It had a nose that could smell a steak cooking in Canada. And the same zit on its forehead.

Between them was a sign with big, black letters.

PRESENTING
Bado I and Bado II
Discovered recently in the

117

Hoosickill River near the
site of Badoglio's
Wakefield home

And under the big letters it said:

> THESE EARLY WORKS, THOUGH INCOMPLETE AND SAD-
> LY ERODED, WILL BE INVALUABLE TO BADOGLIO
> SCHOLARS EVERYWHERE IN THE STUDY OF HIS EVO-
> LUTION AS A SCULPTOR. RESIDENTS OF WAKEFIELD
> HAVE MUCH REASON TO BE PROUD.

I could feel the blood draining out of my head, and I
grabbed a silver post to steady myself. I couldn't believe
it. I figured I must have been dreaming. Nightmaring.

Still hanging onto the post, I turned and looked at Mom.
She was studying the head Lymie made, the one she hadn't
seen yet, and she was wearing one of those idle half smiles
that people wear when they look at sunsets and sleeping
babies and stuff. I held my breath while she gave it a good
going over, praying when she got to mine she wouldn't
recognize it.

She took a step forward and spotted my head. She kept
that same smile for about five seconds. Then I sensed a
change. In the eyes first, I think. Then her body kind
of stiffened. Then the smile faded like lights at a movie
theater, only about ten times slower. By the time she turned
her gaze on me that smile was history.

"All those heads looked kinda the same, huh Mom?"
I stammered, all bug-eyed. "It's like you can't tell one
from . . ."

"You . . ." That was the only word I actually heard her
say. Then I was pretty sure she made this little squeaking
sound—the same kind of sound I made one time when
Lymie slammed me on my back when we were wrestling
and knocked the wind out of me. But maybe she didn't.
It might have just been the way she looked. But she did
put this death grip on my arm, and the next thing I knew

118

I was being pulled out of line and pushed toward the exit. We were moving so fast the guard at the door jumped in front of us to make sure we weren't stealing a picture or anything. When he saw the look on my face, he probably decided I was getting ready to barf all over the trailer, and he jumped back out of our way.

Before I knew it I was being towed across the park. Pretty soon we came to a bench. Mom pushed me onto it and sat next to me. I stared straight ahead, afraid to move a muscle. I could hear Mom breathing and I know it sounds stupid but I swear to God I could feel anger radiating off her like static electricity. Nobody said anything. It was one of those awkward silences that seem to go on forever.

I closed my eyes. And groaned. Only inside, without making a peep. I was too scared to even think of doing my puppy face.

I opened my eyes. Then I cranked them to the side without
moving my head. Mom was still there. What did I expect?
When I straightened out my eyes, I spotted Lymie and
Toddie Phillips walking across the park. They stopped and
snooped around some of the tables, probably looking for
early signs of food, and then shuffled off toward the trailer.
From the way they were acting you could tell they hadn't
seen me get dragged out of there. Part of me hoped they'd
see me and come over to our bench, and part of me hoped
they wouldn't. If they came over, Mom *might* feel like she
had to be nicer. On the other hand, she might be so mad
this time she wouldn't care who was around, and I'd end
up being humiliated in front of two of my friends. Anyway,
it didn't matter. Lymie and Toddie got into the trailer line
without even seeing us.

I wasn't sure what to do—wait for Mom to start in on
me, or maybe start right in apologizing. I didn't dare start
throwing excuses around. In the state Mom was in, that'd
be like throwing fuel onto a fire. If I looked like I was
about to cry, that might help some. But even if she got
softened up enough to listen to some excuses, I still wasn't

home free. The best excuse I could think of was to tell her that when Chuckie laughed at our heads, we were really hurt. And then I could say that when I heard Mom herself laughing at our heads before she even saw them, that kind of pushed us over the edge. We were so ashamed, we *had* to get rid of them. I mean, if your own mother laughs at you. . . . The only problem was that excuse didn't explain why we had to chuck them in the exact spot where we knew they'd be dredging for the Badoglio heads. That'd be tough to explain. Maybe impossible. And I knew that just saying, "We thought it'd be funny" wouldn't do the trick either.

I turned my head in slow motion and slid my eyes around to study Mom's face. I couldn't tell much. She just looked like maybe somebody was pinching her real hard.

I waited and thought some more. A couple of times Mom seemed like she might be on the verge of saying something, but then she'd shake her head and think better of it. She was probably playing around with different hollers, same as I was playing around with different excuses. I wondered who'd end up going first. It didn't look like it'd be me. I couldn't come up with a reason why we'd chucked the heads where we did.

Mom started. Finally.

"I would like . . ." She stopped and took a deep breath. Her voice was so quiet I had to really listen. Like she was holding back, afraid she might grab my throat or something. "I would like it . . . very much . . . if you could tell me . . . what those *things* of yours . . . are doing on display . . . in that trailer." She was getting into a rhythm now and picking up the pace. "Hundreds of people . . ." She jerked her finger toward the trailer. "Hundreds of people will be filing through that trailer, and what do you suppose they expect to see? Tell me that!"

I shrugged. "Art?" I squeaked.

"Not to mention the reporters who'll be arriving later . . . photographers, TV crews, more art critics . . . and what do you suppose they'll all expect to see? Tell me that!" She was starting to let out all the stops.

"Mom, calm down," I said and looked around. "I already told you."

"They think they're seeing . . ."

"Mom, you're getting all hyper," I said, looking around some more. "You're gonna make a scene . . ."

"They think," she said, slower and quieter, "they think they're seeing *art . . .*"

"That's what I said."

"Please don't interrupt. Let me finish. Those people . . ." She waved her arms at the growing crowd around the trailer. "Those people think they're seeing the most priceless treasure that has ever come from this town. They think they're seeing history being made. They think . . ." She ran out of steam.

"They're happy," I ventured weakly.

"Happy? *Happy?* And how long do you think they'll stay that way after they find out that their precious treasures were hammered out by delinquents in my garage!" She gave kind of a shiver when she said that.

I waited to see if she was done yelling for a while. She seemed to be.

"Delinquents is a little strong, isn't it, Mom?" If I could get her to feel guilty, I might have a chance.

She didn't answer. It was like I hadn't said anything. Then she looked at me.

"How could you do something like that?"

I looked at her to see if she wanted an answer or if she was only yelling some more.

"Well?"

She wanted an answer.

"You and Chuckie laughed at us. So we threw them away." I studied her face.

"Threw them *away?*" She looked puzzled. Then she gave me this *I know thirteen years ago I must have brought home the wrong baby from the hospital* look. "Away means . . ." She swung her arm out wide and I flinched. "Away . . .

gone . . . out of reach. It's not throwing them *away* when you put them exactly where you know they'll be found by the dredging team!"

I squirmed and looked down at the ground. "I think 'away' is kinda general. You know, like when a person gets rid of something, he throws it *away* and it doesn't really have anything to do with who finds it or anything." When I get nervous, I babble. And when I babble, I get more nervous. "So when we threw those things away . . ."

Mom was giving me another *wrong baby* look. "Tyler, forget the word 'away.' That's not the point. The point is . . ." She waved her finger in my face. "The point is . . ." She kept waving her finger even though she didn't seem too sure what the point was anymore. "Those people . . ." She stuck her finger toward the trailer. "Those people think those heads—your heads—are valuable works of art. The pride and joy of the town!" She threw up her hands. "Art critics will be using those heads to further their understanding of Badoglio. Using *your* heads!"

"You always say *I* should use my head." Another thing I do when I get nervous: make dumb jokes.

"Don't you *dare* try to be funny, young man. This is serious business."

"But, Mom," I whined. "If you look at it right, it *is* kind of a joke. You know, like funny. A little." I searched her face for some sign of appreciation. No such luck.

"A joke? A *joke*!" She popped off the bench and started pacing up and down in front of me. Then she poked her face in mine. "A joke is something people laugh at! A joke is something people enjoy! Do you honestly think that anybody will *laugh* at this? Do you think that anybody will *enjoy* this?" She stood up straight and looked down at me.

"Chuckie did."

"Chuckie?" Her eyes kind of bugged out. And she stuck her face down by mine again. "You mean to say *Chuckie* knew about this?" She stood up straight again and got that indignant look she gets sometimes.

123

Bad move. I shouldn't've thrown Chuckie in.

"Well, he doesn't really *know* about it. Not really. He kind of does, but he didn't actually . . ."

"Stop," Mom said. "Right now. Stop. You're doing it again. You're making me crazy."

"Sorry."

"I wonder sometimes if you don't do this to me deliberately to try to slip out of situations."

"Mom, believe it or not, I don't like this any better than you do. I don't know what to do."

"You don't know what to do? Isn't it a little late to be worrying about that? Why didn't you . . ."

"Mom, don't keep yelling. I'm scared enough as it is." I looked at the ground. "You thought I was upset all week about the Keepouts. That was part of it. But most of it was this. I thought about this all week. I even dreamed about it."

It was quiet for a long time. Then she sat down next to me.

"Tyler, why on earth didn't you come to me and tell me? What's a parent for?"

"I was afraid."

"Afraid?" She said it like she couldn't believe it. She picked up my head and made me look at her. "I'm your mother. How could you be afraid of your own mother? Have I ever done anything to make you afraid of me?"

"I was afraid you'd carry on like you were just carrying on. I hate it when I make you get like that." I pulled my head away and looked back down at the ground. "You never get like that around anybody else. You're always calm and happy, except for when I start doing things . . ."

Mom stood up and started pacing again. I could see her feet going back and forth. Then I felt her arm on my shoulder and she sat by me again.

"I worry about you, honey. I'm sorry, but I do. And when I get worried, I get upset. And when I get upset . . ."

"It's not your fault," I said. "I don't *blame* you for getting mad. Who wouldn't?"

"Tyler, even if I get upset . . . even if I yell a little, that shouldn't stop you from coming to me when you're worried about something or you need something."

"I already ruined your last two weekends," I said. "First with what we did to Reginald. Then the Keepout thing. I didn't think it was a good time to come to you and tell you about the heads. I was just hoping and praying that the whole thing would blow over."

Mom smiled. "You know, every week when your brother calls, the first thing he wants to know is what you've been up to. And when I hear myself telling him, I sometimes can't believe my own ears. I don't know what there is about you, but I can always count on something happening when you're around. I never know what it'll be, so I can never quite prepare myself for it. Sometimes I wake up with a start in the middle of the night just wondering what your devious little mind will come up with next. And it scares me. It really does. But you know what? I wouldn't trade you for all the peace of mind in the world." She paused and rubbed my shoulder. "Tyler, don't you know that even if I yell at you, even if I turn purple and scream into your face, it doesn't matter. Things won't change between us." She pulled my head up and made me look at her. "I'm crazy about you. I can't help it."

I thought for a minute. "So you don't mind when I do stupid things? You kinda like it?"

Mom got me in a headlock and gave me a noogie. "Don't push your luck," she told me.

Lymie and Toddie came out the other side of the trailer. They were so far away I couldn't see the looks on their faces. Lymie probably still thought we'd be safe if we kept our mouths shut. And because of that Toddie probably still didn't even know what was going on. I watched them wander back over toward the tables and sniff around some more for food. When they didn't find any, they headed off behind the trailer exhibit.

Right then I saw Chuckie step out of the trailer. I hadn't even seen him go in. I wondered what he was thinking. He looked around until he spotted us. For a second he looked like he might make a run for it. Then he started our way.

"Hey, Mom. Here comes Chuckie."

"Good," Mom said. "Since *he's* had longer to think about this, maybe *he'll* know what to do about it."

"Don't count on it, Mom. He's the one that told me not to worry because the critics would never be dumb enough to think those things were genuine."

We sat there not saying anything until Chuckie got up to us.

"Hey, Chuckie," I said, "those critics are a lot dumber than we figured."

"So I noticed." He sat down next to me.

"The poor kid," Mom said and started rubbing my head. "He's been upset about this all week."

Chuckie looked at me sitting there getting my head rubbed. First he gave me a little smirk, then he put his hands up like puppy paws and scrunched up his face to look pathetic.

I gave him a dirty look. "Shut up, Chuckie. I didn't even do that."

"Aarff, aarff," Chuckie said and laughed.

I punched him. Mom looked at both of us like we were crazy.

"If you two *children* would cut out whatever it is you're doing, we do have some important decisions to make."

We all sat around for a few minutes, nobody saying anything.

"Maybe . . ." My voice sounded little and squeaky. "I don't know, maybe we should just leave it the way it is. They're happy . . ." I pointed toward the people coming out of the trailer. "And me and Lymie aren't in trouble yet. And you're not publicly humiliated or anything yet, Mom . . . I mean, why rock the boat?"

"Rock the boat?" Mom said. "Rock the boat? I think the boat has already been rocked. Royally! Would you rather wait a month or so until somebody decides to auction those heads for a few hundred thousand dollars? And *then* somebody finds out they're not genuine, and the police are called in, and . . ."

"Mom, come on. Don't go hyper again. I was only giving a suggestion. Geez."

Mom put her arm around me and scrunched me up close to her. "I'm sorry," she said.

"Good move, Ace," Chuckie said and gave me the thumbs up.

I gave him an elbow.

We sat around for another minute. Then I looked up at Mom.

"You think they could really get a few hundred thousand for our heads?"

"Could be," Mom said. "Collectors pay big money for works by well-known artists."

"Wow." I shook my head and thought. "Hey, Mom. I was wondering. You looked at both those heads pretty good. Which one do you think would bring in more money—the one I did or the one Lymie did?"

"I don't believe you, Tyler!" She pulled her arm out from around me. "That's all you can think of? Everything is always a competition between you boys, isn't it? Who's stronger? Who's smarter? Who's braver? . . ."

"That's easy, Mom. Me." I tried to give a little laugh.

She wasn't amused. All that sympathy I'd been getting evaporated. Mom glared at me. I heard Chuckie snort.

"I was kidding, Mom! Kidding. You know, a joke, ha, ha."

She didn't ha, ha. She glared at me another minute and then leaned up to talk to Chuckie. "Chuckie, you haven't said much. What do you think?"

Chuckie leaned back on the bench and stretched his feet out across the grass. He shook his head. "I don't know, Ms. L. I never thought it would go this far. I mean, how could they have thought those things were genuine? I thought they were supposed to be experts."

"Well, that's another question for another day," Mom said. "Now we have to decide what to do about the situation at hand. Any ideas?"

Mom and I leaned forward, our eyes beading into Chuckie's face.

"Look," Chuckie said after a while. "Who's gonna be most humiliated about this whole fiasco? Who's got the most to lose?"

"Me," I said. "Me and Lymie."

"Nope," Chuckie said. "You're just a couple of kids. Kids always do crazy things. People expect it. They won't really blame you."

"They'll blame me," Mom said. "They'll think I'm a bad mother. And Lymie's poor parents. Those poor people don't even know about this yet." She shook her head sadly.

I patted Mom's knee. "You're a good mother, Mom. Your whole life you've tried to stop me from doing stupid things."

"No, no, no," Chuckie said. "Let me finish. Nobody's gonna blame you, Ms. L. This guy . . ." He jerked his thumb at me. "This guy has got to be one of the politest kids in town. Everybody always says that. I mean, this kid says 'excuse me' if he walks *behind* somebody in the super-market aisle, for crying out loud." He smiled and poked me.

"Well, they might turn around, and then I'd be walking in front of them," I said.

"You see?" Chuckie said. "You see what I mean? Nobody'll say you didn't raise him right. And nobody'll blame the Lawrences either. Lymie's never been in any real trouble. Why, most people would trust Lymie with their . . ." He groped the air with his hands. "Well, I don't know if they'd trust him with anything all that important, but they'd trust him."

"Yeah," I said, "so what are you saying?"

"Go back to my original question, Ace. Who's got the most to lose?"

"I don't know, Chuckie. Why don't you just . . ."

128

"The critics!" Mom yelled. "The art critics have the most to lose. They'll be disgraced when this comes out!"

"Right!" Chuckie said. "Right!"

"Oh, those poor men!" Mom said. "We'll ruin those poor men."

"Well, don't feel too bad," Chuckie said. "They've ruined a few people themselves. They make and break new artists every week by what they say about them."

"Yeah," I said. "You shoulda seen the way they acted the other night, Mom. Like they really thought they were hot stuff."

"Tyler," Mom said, "they don't deserve *this*. No matter how smug . . ."

"Wait," Chuckie said. "You didn't let me finish again. Nobody needs to be disgraced. See, they can make the announcement themselves. They can say that upon closer observation they discovered that the heads were imitations—clever imitations maybe, but imitations. They apologize for the mistake. People might be a little disappointed, but they still go on thinking that the critics must be pretty smart for being able to tell when a work of art is phony. So you see, nobody loses."

"Wow," I said. "You're right." I turned to Mom. "He's right. This is great! Nobody's gonna have to worry about anything."

"Not till we get home anyway," Mom said to me. Then to Chuckie, "I'm so glad you're here, Chuckie." She took a deep breath and shook her head. "When I saw that head sitting there . . ." She gave a little shudder. "I had no idea what we were going to do. I really didn't."

"Well, we're not completely out of the woods yet," Chuckie said. "First we have to convince those critics that these guys made the heads. But that shouldn't be too hard. The two of them can tell how they made them, and we can say how we saw them before they were dredged up."

"Oh, look," Mom said. "There's Lymie's mother. I'd better fill her in on all this. She'll probably want to be with us when we go to sort this all out."

"Mom, I . . ."

"I'll be right back, hon. Don't worry. We'll all go with you. Everything will be fine."

She was off. I looked at Chuckie.

"Chuckie, I really don't want this to be some kind of mob scene. It'll be bad enough confessing to those critics without our mothers standing behind us. I mean, that'll just add to the embarrassment."

Chuckie nodded. "You want me to go with you, Ace?"

"Yeah, I do," I said. "But I don't know if Mom would understand. She might feel bad if I want you to go but not her."

"Yeah, maybe," Chuckie said. "You think you and Lymie can handle it on your own?"

I looked across the park to where Mom was jabbering away at Mrs. Lawrence. Lymie's little sister Susan, who's five going on forty, was standing next to her mother with her arms folded, taking it all in. Luckily, Lymie's little brothers Larry and Lonnie weren't around, or they might've run off and blabbed to everybody what was going on. I watched Mrs. Lawrence. First her hands were down by her sides. Then they were on her hips. And by the time Mom got done, she looked like she was rolling up her sleeves for a street brawl or something. I could almost hear her saying something like, "When I get my hands on *him* . . ." Lymie'd be lucky if he didn't end up getting chased around the park and belted in front of the whole town.

"Yeah," I said, "we'll handle it."

And I took off to find Lymie before his mother did.

16

"You jerk!"

Lymie pushed me hard and I almost landed on my butt.

"What do you mean, *me* jerk? This is *your* fault!"

I pushed him hard and almost landed on my butt again.

"You told!" Lymie yelled. "I can't believe you told!"

"Told what?" Toddie wanted to know.

"I didn't tell, you idiot! Why don't you just *listen* for once in your stupid life?"

I went to push him again, but he grabbed my arm and cranked it behind my back. Then he stuck his foot in front of my foot and kept cranking until I was face down in the dirt.

"Don't call me an idiot, sleaze bucket! I'm sicka you calling me an idiot!"

I bobbed my head up. " 'CAUSE YOU ARE AN IDI-OT!"

Lymie scrunched my head down with his other hand until my nose and mouth were pressed so hard against the damp, packed dirt I could hardly breathe. I closed my eyes and squirmed like crazy until I thought my arm would pop out of its socket.

"Leggoa his head, Lyme! He's sucking up dirt."

He let go of my head, and when I opened my eyes, I saw Toddie's face down by mine like some referee at a wrestling match.

"Told what?" Toddie said.

I spit out some dirt and Toddie backed off a little. "I didn't tell anybody anything!"

Toddie's head floated up toward Lymie. "Then what are *you* so mad about?"

"He got me in trouble!" Lymie yelled. " 'Cause he's got a BIG MOUTH!" He cranked on my arm some more.

"Look, you id . . ." I stopped and took a deep breath. "Look, Lymie, my mother saw the head I made and almost had a heart attack. She'd seen it already when it was still at my house."

"Then why'd you show it to her? You like getting in trouble or something?" He scrunched my head down a couple more times, bouncing my ear on the dirt.

"Hey, what are you doing to him? Get off!" It was a girl's voice.

I felt Lymie get off. When I rolled over, I saw that Babette had him by the collar. Mary Grace was gawking down at me all bug-eyed. Toddie looked more confused than ever.

I got up on my elbows and glared at Lymie. "How was I supposed to know you were gonna get the big idea to chuck those things in the river? This is all your own fault!" I leaned in toward him. "Idiot."

Lymie pulled toward me like a mean dog on a leash. Babette held fast.

"Tyler," Mary Grace said, kind of stepping in between us, "what are you talking about? And why are you two trying to kill each other?"

"Somebody told something," Toddie said, and everybody glared at him.

I climbed to my feet and started brushing myself off.

"Go ahead, big mouth," Lymie said. "You might as well tell everybody. I know you're gonna eventually."

"Lymie," I said, sticking my face in his, "there's no sense talking to you. You're totally unreasonable. You don't know logic. You wouldn't know logic if it hit you over the head. You're a nut case!"

"Bigmouth!"

Babette let go of Lymie and pushed him away from me. Then she turned to me.

"Tell."

"If I tell, he'll say I'm a bigmouth."

"Tell!" She made a fist and glared into my face.

"All right, all right." I pushed her fist down. "I'll tell. But first you gotta all promise not to say a word. Not to anybody."

"It seems funny to hear *you* say that," Lymie said.

"Shut up," Babette said. "We promise. Now tell."

I bent over and shook some dirt out of my hair. Then I looked at Babette and Mary Grace. "Have you been in the trailer yet?"

They said yes.

"So you saw those new heads Badoglio supposedly made?"

They said yes.

"Well . . ." I felt around my nose. "Well, Badoglio didn't make those heads. Me and Lymie did."

You could've heard a pin drop. Everybody except Lymie looked at everybody else and then back at me.

"No way!" Babette said.

"Tyler!" Mary Grace said.

"But the sign said Badoglio made 'em," Toddie said.

"*Toddie*," I said, trying to keep my patience. "Yeah, the sign *said* Badoglio made them. Because everybody thinks Badoglio made them. But Badoglio didn't make them. Me and Lymie did. And we threw them in the river. And . . ."

"Why?" Mary Grace said.

"I don't know," I said. "It was one of el Idiota's bright ideas." I jerked my thumb at Lymie.

"And the tattletot here had to go and squeal," Lymie sneered. "And now *his* mother told *my* mother the whole

133

story. And I'll probably get grounded for the rest of my life!"

"Don't call me tattletot, jerk!" I stepped toward him. Babette stuck her hand on my chest and pushed me back. I stood there glaring over her shoulder at Lymie. Then I told the rest of them, "My mother saw my head the day I made it. And when she recognized it in the trailer, she went nuts."

"Wow," everybody said except Lymie and me.

"And then Chuckie came up with a plan that might get us out of trouble. And my mother saw Lymie's mother walk by and she wanted to discuss it with her."

"And I'm dead," Lymie said. He reached over to push me again, but without any gusto. Lymie has such a short attention span.

Lymie and I went back to the bench where our mothers were sitting so we could make sure they were going to let us take care of everything on our own. We told Mary Grace and Babette and Toddie we'd be back in a few minutes. Chuckie was talking to Mom and Mrs. Lawrence, and Lymie's sister Susan was right there listening with this serious look on her face. They didn't even see us until we were standing right in front of them.

"What on earth happened to you?" Mom said. She stood up and started brushing crud out of my hair and out of my ear and off my face.

Lymie's mother jumped up and looked like she might backhand Lymie. "AS IF YOU'RE NOT IN ENOUGH TROUBLE ALREADY!" She yanked him around and plunked him down on the bench next to Chuckie.

"I'm all right," I said, pulling away from Mom. "I got dirt on my head. Big deal."

"Look," Chuckie said, "we don't have a whole lot of time. Right now the art critics are still at Mrs. Hildegarde's. But if you guys wait too long, they'll be *here*, surrounded by people."

I didn't want that to happen. I figured those guys would

probably turn out to be emotional artistic types who'd start running around in circles and screaming at us like banshees. It'd be bad enough in private. "Let's go, Lyme." I gave a little tug to his shirt.

Mom looked us both over. "Boys, are you sure you don't want us to go with you? For moral support?"

"No, Mom. It's our problem. We'll handle it."

"And if they don't believe you," Chuckie said, "come back and get me. I'll be right here."

"We'll *all* be right here," Mrs. Lawrence said.

I heard Lymie groan.

Mary Grace and Babette and Toddie were waiting for us at the other side of the park. We told them what we had to do.

"They're not going to believe us," Lymie said. "I can tell you that right now. You shoulda made Chuckie come with us."

"You don't *make* Chuckie do anything," I told him. "And if we tried, we'd've got stuck going over there with our mothers. Is that what you wanted, Lyme?"

"Forget it," Lymie said. "Let's just get this over with."

We started trudging down the street, Lymie and I in the lead. Mrs. Hildegarde's house was just around the corner on Main Street.

"What are you going to say?" Babette darted in front of me and studied my face.

I shrugged. "I don't know. We're gonna tell them what we did."

"But how are you gonna start? I mean, are you gonna barge in there yelling, 'We chiseled those heads,' or what? You oughta know what you're gonna say so you don't end up looking like total jerks."

She was right. Lymie and I looked at each other.

"I'm not that good on my feet," I said. "I get all nervous and I ramble. Maybe you should do the talking, Lyme."

"Nice try, Ty, but no way. You're the one who's supposed to be the brain, remember? Besides, you're smaller and more pathetic-looking, so you probably won't get belted or anything."

"Thanks, Lymie. You're a real pal."

"He does have a point," Babette said.

I gave her a dirty look.

"No," she said. "I don't mean that as an insult. It's just that you do have the kind of face that'd be hard for an adult to scream at very long."

"Yeah?" I said. "That just sounds like a polite way of saying I'm pathetic-looking."

"I think Babette means you have a sensitive face," Mary Grace said. "And that's good."

"Yeah," Babette said. "And with that face, I bet if you started crying you'd have it made in the shade. They'd probably offer to go out and buy you ice cream or something."

"He was crying at the Keepouts' and it didn't do him any good," Lymie said.

Babette poked him. She didn't want me to see, but I did.

"I was only trying to make a point," Lymie said.

"The Keepouts aren't normal," Babette said. "So your point is stupid."

"And you're telling me those critics are normal?" Lymie said.

Then Mary Grace got into it again. "I think you should just go up to them and tell the truth. Don't worry about putting on a big act."

We all looked at her like she had two heads or something. You could tell she'd never been in trouble before.

If I was scared walking over to Mrs. Hildegarde's house, it was nothing compared to how I felt when I got there. Lymie didn't show it, but I think he was pretty well shook too.

"Well," Babette said, "you might as well get in there and get it over with."

"Yeah," Lymie said and gave me a shove. "Let's go."

"*You* go," I said and gave him a shove.

"Look, Ty," Lymie told me. "You knock on the door. Mrs. Hildegarde answers and says, "Oh, it's that polite McAllister boy and his good-looking friend!" He stood up straight and pursed his lips the way he figured Mrs. Hildegarde would. "Then when you're inside, you go over to the two art critics and say, 'I'm very sorry. I've done something very bad. I made those heads and I'm really sorry.' Then if they look like they're gonna belt you or scream at you or something, you cry. What's so tough about that?"

"Real funny, Lyme. And you really expect me to say *I* made the heads? What about you?"

"All right, all right. Say 'we.' Who cares about one little proposition?"

"That's preposition, goofis. And when it comes to confessions, I do."

"You're both wrong," Babette said. "It's a pronoun."

Lymie pointed in my face and laughed. "See," he said, "you *don't* know everything."

I looked at both of them. Then at Mary Grace. "They think this is a grammar class. I'm so nervous I can't think straight, and they're worried about whether I know pronouns." I turned to Lymie. "*Which I do.*"

"All right, Ty. Good. You know your pronouns." He said it smug like he was an adult talking to some little kid. "But you gotta relax so you can do this right. Do what they always tell you in speech classes. Picture those guys in their underwear."

"Please," Babette groaned. "You're gonna make the kid get sick."

I took one last deep breath and hoped my face was as pathetic-looking as everybody said it was.

"Well, here goes."

In the middle of my first step, I heard tires screech and a horn go off. I turned and saw Buster in his big old Cadillac with the front end still bobbing. He leaned over and cranked down his passenger window.

"Hey, McAllister, what are you, some kinda art groupie or something?" He blew cigar smoke out at me.

"Oh, great," I mumbled, but not so Buster could hear me. I went over to his window. "Hi, Buster. What are you doing here?"

He shrugged. "I'm just driving by and I see all you hanging around in front of Hildegarde's house and I think to myself, 'What are they up to?' It made me wonder, you know, like do we live in a world that's so screwed up that kids these days are hanging around waiting for autographs from those two art bozos in there? So I turn around and come back 'cause I had to find out. Call me a student of human nature." He chomped down on his cigar and took a couple of puffs.

"Nah," I said. "We don't want their autographs." I tried to smile.

"What do you need, some advice on a tree you drew in art class or something?" He yanked the cigar out of his mouth and let loose with a big belly laugh. "That's rich!"

"Nah," I said and looked at the ground.

"It's a secret," Toddie said.

Buster's eyes twinkled up at Toddie. "Who's got a secret?"

"Lymie and Tyler."

We both groaned.

"A secret, huh?" Buster's eyes got bigger. He opened his door and hoisted himself up out of his seat. Then he came around the front of his car to where we were and put one arm around my shoulders and one arm around Lymie's and scrunched us in close to him. "We don't have any secrets from each other now, do we boys?"

"No." I heard Lymie's voice coming from the other side of Buster.

"It's not really a secret," I said. I looked over at Babette and she rolled her eyes. Mary Grace wasn't any help either. "It's more of a private thing."

"McAllister, I'm surprised at you." I could tell he was looking down at me because thick smoke was swirling around my face. "There's nothing private between friends, is there? Huh?" He scrunched me in closer. "You guys do consider old Buster your friend, don't you? I mean, if you didn't, I'd be crushed." On the word "crushed" he really squished me hard so that half my face was buried in fat.

"Yeah," I said.

"Yeah," I heard Lymie say.

"Well, then, let's get it out in the open. Let's share our problem with good old Uncle Buster." He scooped me up in his arm and set me on his car hood. Before I knew it, Lymie was sitting there beside me. "Well?"

"The thing is, Buster . . ." I looked to Lymie for help. He was staring at Buster wide-eyed with his mouth open. I might as well have been sitting by a guppy. "The thing is . . . this is something that's, I don't know, it's kind of . . . you might say, delicate, I guess, and it can't get out."

"McAllister, McAllister, McAllister." Buster patted my knee. "Say no more. Surely you don't think old Uncle Buster'd be indiscreet. Is that what you think?"

That's the thing about Buster. One minute he'll talk like a slob, and then he'll turn around and use a word like "indiscreet." It makes it hard to tell who you're talking to.

"No," I said and squirmed around on the hood. "I don't think you're indiscreet."

"So let's have it." Buster poked his head down next to mine. He looked like Wile E. Coyote whenever he's sure he's finally got the Roadrunner.

I gulped and looked at Lymie. He shrugged. Buster's face moved in closer and seemed to be saying, "I don't have all day, kid."

"You know those heads they found?" I began weakly.

"Yeah." Buster pulled in even closer and puffed a few times.

Being scared makes me sick. And cigar smoke makes me sick. I was afraid I'd throw up on him.

"Me and Lymie made them," I blurted out. Buster pulled

139

away and straightened up. I took a humongous deep breath of fresh air.

Buster looked down and studied my face. Then he studied Lymie's face.

"You're lying," he said.

I just stared at him. I could hardly breathe.

"We're always telling him not to lie," Babette said. "But you don't listen, *do you, Tyler?*" Her eyes were bugging out the way my mother's do when I do something wrong in public.

"No," I squeaked and looked at the ground.

More smoke swirled around my head. Buster was moving in on me again.

"No." He said it like he was in awe. "No, the kid's telling the truth. Aren't you, McAllister? You're telling the truth."

I looked to Lymie for help. He sat frozen like a statue, his eyes fixed on Buster. I looked at Babette and Mary Grace. Babette shrugged and Mary Grace tried to smile. I didn't even bother looking at Toddie.

Buster was down in my face again. My head was in the middle of a smoke cloud. I held my breath and felt my eyes water.

"You guys did make those heads, didn't you, McAllister?"

I nodded. When Buster straightened up again, I breathed. And looked around. Everybody was staring at Buster.

Buster took a couple of steps back, looked at me again, and then looked over at Mrs. Hildegarde's house. Slowly a smile appeared on his lips. The smile grew into a grin and the grin into a chuckle. Then all the layers of fat on Buster began to shake, and he began to roar. With laughter, that is. He laughed so hard he started to cough and then he looked like he might be choking or something. His huge body pitched forward over the hood of his car. Lymie and I scrambled out of his way and jumped to the ground. Then we all just stood there staring at him laughing and gasping for all he was worth. Every once in a while he'd catch his breath enough to say a word, and every time it'd

140

be the same word. Finally he stood up, sighed, wiped his eyes, and looked at Mrs. Hildegarde's house again. Then he smiled and said that same word again.

"Beautiful!"

"You gotta big mouth!"

Lymie stomped his feet into the ground and screamed into my face like I was a major league umpire or something. I didn't say anything. I felt too terrible.

"Leave him alone, Lymie," Mary Grace said. "What'd you expect him to do with a five-hundred-pound guy squeezing him?"

"Yeah, and we didn't see you do anything heroic," Babette said. "You sat there looking like your eyes were gonna pop out of your head."

"But I kept my mouth shut!" Lymie yelled. "I didn't spill my guts!" He looked at Toddie. "And *you*! Why'd you have to tell Buster we had a secret?"

"I didn't tell him what it was," Toddie said.

"Well, it's done now," Mary Grace said. "So why keep yelling about it?"

"Yeah, shut up," Babette said.

We walked along for another few minutes with nobody saying anything.

"I'm sorry," I said miserably.

"What?" Lymie barked.

"He said he was sorry," Babette told him. "Are you deaf or something?"

"Aha!" Lymie said. "So he admits he did something wrong!"

"Shut up," Babette said. And then to me, "Tyler, don't sweat it. Buster said he'd take care of everything."

"Hmmph," I said.

"Look," Mary Grace said. "You and Lymie were dreading going into that house to talk to those critics. And now you don't have to. Buster couldn't wait to run in and tell them. Maybe Buster was a blessing in disguise."

"Hmmph," I said.

"It stinks," Lymie said. "Our whole entire future is in the hands of Buster Rudzinski!"

"Come on," Mary Grace said. "Let's have a little faith in human nature. Buster said he'd take care of everything, so why don't we leave it at that. There's nothing we can do about it now anyway."

"Hmmph," I said.

"Hey," Babette said. "Can you picture him? Buster's probably in there right now laughing his head off, rolling around on Mrs. Hildegarde's floor, telling those guys what fools they are." She started laughing. "He's probably turning purple and dropping cigar ashes all over Mrs. Hildegarde's rug. Can't you just see the look on her face?"

I tried to picture Mrs. Hildegarde in there with Buster. I mean, she was a woman who thought it was undignified to have a *TV* in her house.

Suddenly Lymie burst out laughing and punched my arm.

"Hey, Ty," he said, "can't you just see those two art geeks in there? That little spastic one's probably twitching his face off by now."

I had to smile. I couldn't help it. "And the fat one's probably busting all the buttons off his sport coat," I said and looked up at everybody. They were all laughing, even Mary Grace and Toddie.

"We shoulda sneaked up to the window and peeked in,"

Lymie said. "I can't believe we didn't do that. How come we didn't thinka that, Ty?"

"Probably because you were screaming in his face," Babette said, and we all started laughing all over again.

Mom and Mrs. Lawrence and Chuckie were there waiting for us on the bench. Susan was out in front pretending to be a ballerina. When our mothers saw us laughing, they looked like they didn't know whether to be mad or relieved.

"Well?" Mom said. You could tell she didn't think anything was so funny.

"No sweat, Mom," I said. "Everything is A-okay."

"So you told them?" Chuckie said, looking a little puzzled. "What'd they say?"

I looked at Lymie. I wasn't going to tell them the whole story and have Lymie call me a bigmouth. Lymie poked me and nodded. Mary Grace and Babette and Toddie all gave a little giggle.

"We don't know," I said. "That's what we're laughing about."

The three of them on the bench gave each other the eye. Then they gave us the eye.

"This I gotta hear," Chuckie said and stood up. Mom and Mrs. Lawrence stood up too, and Susan stopped dancing. Lymie slipped around behind me, probably so it'd be harder for his mother to get her hands on him.

"This better be good," Mrs. Lawrence said and folded her arms.

"Real good," Mom said and folded her arms.

I could feel my smile fading away. Under the glare of all those eyes, the idea of letting Buster take care of our head problem suddenly seemed stupid. Incredibly stupid. Like the dumbest thing anybody's ever done in the whole history of the world. I looked at Lymie. He'd lost his smile too. And Mary Grace and Babette and Toddie didn't look so enthused anymore either.

I sighed. And I caught myself giving my puppy look without even meaning to.

144

Lymie crammed another hot dog into his mouth. He was in food booth heaven. He'd already downed two sugar fritters, three slices of pizza, and a walkaway sundae.

"I wish I could be like that," I said to the others.

"Are you kidding?" Babette said. "You want to be a human garbage disposal?"

I smiled. "No, but look at him. He doesn't even get upset. I mean, things like this happen to me and I can't eat for a week. With Lymie, a nuclear bomb could go off in his backyard and he'd probably go out and roast marshmallows on the burning shrubs."

"Who says I don't get upset?" Lymie said and crammed the rest of the hot dog in his mouth. "I just don't see any reason why I should let it interfere with my appetite." Then he belched.

We all looked at him like he was a circus act or something.

"Hey, Ty-wer!"

I turned around and saw Lester Phillips running toward me. And his next-in-line older brother Davy was coming up behind him.

"Hey, Ty-wer!" Lester flew into me, wrapped his arms around my legs, and started swinging around in a circle. I had to grab Lymie's shoulders to keep from tipping over.

"How ya doin', Lester?" I said.

"Aw wight. But they wouldn't wet us in the twailer."

"How come?" I figured maybe they had a dress code or something.

"They locked the doors," Davy said. "It's closed."

I looked at Lymie and Lymie looked at me. We both smiled. Closing the trailer was a good sign. And I thanked God they closed it before Lester got in there and started jumping around and telling everybody how one of the heads was a buddy of his.

"I wonder why they closed it," Toddie said. "There was still a big line."

"I think they're having technical difficulties," I said and winked at Toddie.

Toddie looked confused. "Like on TV?"

I shook my head and pulled him off to the side. I was dragging Lester along too, seeing how he was still kind of attached to my legs. "Toddie, don't you remember what was on display in there?"

He looked over toward the trailer and thought. "Yeah."

"And you remember who made two of those things?"

He thought some more and looked at the trailer again. "Yeah."

"Well, don't you think as soon as the critics found out we made those things, they'd want to shut down the exhibit so nobody else would see 'em?"

Toddie was looking over my shoulder now. Over to where the bandstand was. "Then why'd they just bring them over there?"

"Toddie . . ." I stopped and took a deep breath. Maybe it'd be better just to drop the subject. I looked over to where he was looking. And almost had a heart attack.

"Toddie, take Lester." I unwrapped Lester from around my legs. "Lester, stay here with your brother."

Lester said okay. I took off for the bandstand.

I couldn't believe my eyes. Our two heads were up on a table in front of the bandstand. The skinny critic was hunched down in front of them, and two guards were flanking them. Some other guys were stringing out a chain on some posts to keep back the crowd. Over to the side I saw the fat critic talking to Mrs. Hildegarde. They didn't look all that happy, but they didn't look that upset either.

I crept up as close as I could and peeked around the skinny critic. This ugly thing stared back at me. Lymie's head. Then I saw what the skinny critic was doing. He was hanging the poster that said how genuine our heads were.

"Testing, testing, one, two . . ."

I looked up on the bandstand. And up there tapping on the microphone and wearing this big grin from ear to ear was none other than Buster Rudzinski. He said one last

146

word before he stepped down. He mumbled it, but I knew what it was. The word was "beautiful."

A bunch of guys were busy setting up folding chairs in front of the bandstand, and people were filling up the chairs as fast as they could set them out. A TV 10 news van pulled up and the people inside hopped out and started unloading cameras and mikes and stuff. The mayor and the council guys were making their way up onto the bandstand and filling in the dignitary seats behind the podium. They all looked as proud as could be.

I didn't need to see any more. I ran back to where Lymie and everybody was. As soon as Lester saw me, he came sailing through the air and landed on me, wrapping his arms around my neck and his legs around my sides and yelling "Ty-wer!" in my ear. I teetered over to Lymie.

"Lymie," I said, "We got trouble. Big trouble."

I pointed toward the bandstand. Even from where we were you could make out two stone heads gawking at the gathering crowd. And a third head was beaming out from behind them. Buster's.

"Our heads?" Lymie asked weakly.

"Yeah," I said, "and they got that same poster in front of them saying they're real. Buster never told!"

"I knew it!" Lymie yelled. "I knew it! You're such a jerk, Tyler! I knew we couldn't trust Buster Rudzinski. Now what are you gonna do?"

I looked at him. For about half a minute. Then I clenched my teeth. I walked over to the closest bench, set Lester down, and told him to stay there. And just to be sure he wouldn't wander up to our heads, I told Toddie to watch him. And to be double sure, I told Mary Grace and Babette to watch Toddie. Then I went back to Lymie.

"Look, Lymie, we can discuss this like two rational human beings or I can punch you in the mouth!" I braced myself and pushed him hard. This time he went flying. "I've had it with you! All you do is complain!" I pushed him again and stomped in a circle around him. I noticed a

147

couple of old ladies sitting in seats staring at us, so I latched onto Lymie's arm and towed him out of their range. Lymie just stared at me with his jaw hanging down. He knew this was more than my usual shouting-in-his-face kind of mad. This was *real* mad. "You always criticize whatever I do!" I told him. "You never come up with any ideas on your own! No, wait, I'm wrong! It was your idea for us to make the heads in the first place! And it was your idea to chuck them in the river! And then . . ." I stopped to catch my breath. "And then you blame everything on me! And you call me a bigmouth!" I pushed him again. "And I know what you're doing now. You're waiting for me to come up with an idea. And if it works, good, you'll be happy. And if it doesn't, then you'll tell me how stupid it was. I'm sick of it, Lymie! And I'm sick of you!" I pushed him again, but this time I fell down, right on my butt. And I didn't even bother getting up. I just sat there with my head drooping down between my knees.

I saw Lymie's feet walk up to me. I didn't even care if he wanted to kick me in the head or something.

"Ty?"

"Shut up!"

"Come on, Ty. Hyper down a little." He dropped to his knees. Then he put his hand on my shoulder.

"Get your grubby hands off me," I told him.

"Listen, Ty. Listen to me, will ya?" He grabbed my head and tried to pry it up. "All I want you to do is listen to me. Why you gotta be such a hothead?"

I didn't say anything. And like a little kid, I put my hands over my ears.

Lymie pulled my hands down. "Listen, Ty. How long have you known me? Huh? Tell me that."

"Too long!" I pulled my hands free, but I didn't put them back over my ears again.

"I'll overlook that," Lymie said. "Look, you've known me since the beginning of last summer, right?"

I didn't answer. Lymie reached over and twisted my ears.

148

When I tried to slap his hands away, I almost ripped my ears out by the roots.

"Since the beginning of last summer," he said. "Right?"

"All right!" I yelled, rubbing my ears. "Are you happy now, Lyme?"

"Okay," Lymie said. "And in all that time have I ever once let you down? Haven't I always been right by your side? No matter what?"

"Yeah," I said. "You've been by my side complaining."

"What, you're telling me you never complain? Yeah, I admit I complain once in a while."

"Once in a while?" I finally looked up at him. "That's a laugh."

"All right, so maybe more than once in a while. But I'm always there when you need me, aren't I? Admit it."

I just looked at his dopey face and didn't say anything, so he reached for my ears again.

"Don't!" I said and pulled away.

"Come on. Admit it." Lymie's head was bobbing up and down to show me how he thought I should answer.

"Okay, I admit it."

Lymie's face lit up. "So all right then. Quit complaining. We gotta decide what to do."

I rolled my eyes. "I don't believe it. You always turn everything around to make it look like . . ."

"There you go again, Ty. Complaining."

"Get outta here!" I stood up and brushed myself off. Then I looked back at Lymie kneeling there and wearing this stupid smile. I tried to look mean, but it didn't work. He looked so goofy I could feel my face start to smile.

"Hey, attsa my boy!" Lymie popped up and started thumping me on the back. "Now let's just see what kind of a brilliant plan the old Lyme can come up with."

I looked at him. And he looked like he was really thinking. You could almost see thirteen years' worth of dust rising up from his brain.

It only took Lymie about two minutes to come up with a plan. It called for me to go up to Buster and ask him

149

what was going on. Brilliant. And what would be Lymie's contribution? He'd be right beside me.

As dumb as Lymie's plan was, it was all we had. So we pushed our way through the crowd till we were up against the chain again. The two guards were still in place, but the table with our heads had been moved up on the bandstand. And the row of dignitary chairs had been split, five chairs on each side of the heads. Mrs. Hildegarde had already taken the first seat to the left of Lymie's head, and the two critics were taking seats to the right of my head. The mayor and the council guys who'd been unseated because of the redecorating were scrambling for the other chairs. Buster was back up at the microphone telling everybody to get to their seats so the show could begin. I tried to get his attention without getting everybody else's.

"Hey, kid, look out."

I turned and stuck my face smack dab in the middle of the lens to one of those industrial strength video cameras they use at news stations.

"Smile, kid," said a voice from the other side.

I got out of the way.

"That's the idea," the camera guy said and pointed the camera up at Buster.

When Lymie and I were slinking back to where Mary Grace and Babette and Toddie and Lester and Davy were, an arm reached out from one of the rows of seats and grabbed me. It was attached to Mom. And right next to her was Lymie's mother. Their eyes asked the question.

"Don't worry, Mom," I said. "Everything's cool."

Mom let go of my arm and took a deep breath. "Thank God," she said.

"If I live through this one . . ." Lymie's mother said, and she was kind of waving a fist that I figured had Lymie's name on it. Susan, who was right next to her, started waving a little fist too.

We kept right on going.

"You're getting pretty good," Lymie said. "You never used to be able to lie like that."

"Yeah, well, necessity is the mother of invention."

"Huh?" Lymie said.

Chuckie snagged me before we got to where we were headed, and I told him as much as I knew about what was going on.

He kind of made a whistling noise. "Did you tell your mother?" he wanted to know.

"I lied. I told her everything was fine."

Chuckie shook his head. "What did you go and do that for?"

I shrugged and looked at the ground.

"It's something about a mother of an invention," I heard Lymie tell him.

18

"I'm so happy," Buster began, "to have been asked by our fine panel here to host this afternoon's ceremonies. Delighted." He pursed his lips and said the word "delighted" in a funny voice, the way somebody like Mrs. Hildegarde might've said it. You could see everybody up on the panel wince, like a whip had just cracked two inches behind their heads and they were waiting to see if it'd crack again. "You don't know how proud I am to do my little part to bring a little well-deserved recognition to our fine little town."

"I still can't believe they'd let Buster be the emcee," I whispered to Chuckie. "What are they, crazy or something?"

Lymie and Chuckie and me were sitting under a tree off to the side of the crowd. I didn't feel like being stuck in the middle of what could turn into an angry mob. And if something like that happened, I wanted to make sure we were next to Chuckie.

"Buster's a hard guy to say no to," Chuckie whispered back.

"They're all afraid of him? They think he'd hit 'em or something?"

"It's more like they're afraid of what he'd *say* about them. See, Ace, Buster has this nose for news, and he knows more about everybody in this town than everybody else put together. And whenever Buster has a problem—say he thinks his tax assessment's too high or something—he starts remembering little bits and pieces of information, and pretty soon the problem's taken care of. You know what I mean?"

"So all those people up there have done stuff they're hiding?" I was kind of amazed.

Chuckie looked at me. "I don't know many people who'd want everything they've ever done paraded out for public inspection. Would *you*?"

"Good point," I said. "Right now *I'd* lower his taxes if he wanted me to. Anything just to shut him up."

"How are *you* gonna lower his taxes?" Lymie said, back to his old sarcastic self.

I gritted my teeth. "That was just an example, Lyme."

"Well, it was a stupid one."

I picked up my fist. Chuckie laughed and pushed my hand down. "You guys are amazing," he said.

I looked up at the bandstand. Buster had already introduced the mayor, and he was sitting in a chair he'd pulled up next to the heads, closer to them than anybody. The mayor was saying how there was something special about the people of Wakefield, some special quality that separated them from other folks—call it dedication to a job well done, call it a special vision (he called it a lot of things before he was done)—but his point was that it didn't surprise him at all that these two fine heads, these masterpieces, were chiseled right here in Wakefield. He expected great things to come from Wakefield. And he said how this was only the beginning. He knew Wakefield would continue to generate excellence.

The audience whistled and cheered something fierce. They were still going strong when the mayor sat down. And he didn't sit down all that fast.

"I hate that," I said, "the way politicians always tell

people how great they are just so they can get applause."

"What would you do?" Lymie said. "Tell 'em they're all scumbags?"

Chuckie laughed. And pushed my fist down again.

Every one of the council guys got up and said pretty much the same thing, trying to squeeze out every last ounce of applause. I don't have a whole lot of patience for that kind of thing even on a good day, which this wasn't. I fidgeted, pulling up grass, drumming on my knees, things like that, until Chuckie grabbed my hands and told me to stop.

I leaned back on my elbows. "Hey, Chuckie?"

"Yeah, Ace?"

"What do you think he's up to?"

"Who?"

I popped up off my elbows. "You know who. *Buster.* What's he doing up there? Why didn't he just tell those critics we made the heads?"

Chuckie smirked. "Maybe he was too filled with civic pride to blurt out the truth."

I jabbed his ribs. "Don't be a wise guy, Chuckie. I don't need that now. You know Buster. And I told you how much he laughed when we told him what happened."

"When you told him," Lymie said.

I rolled my eyes. "All right, when I told him. Chuckie, he was going crazy, like it was the funniest thing . . ."

"I know, I know," Chuckie said. "He's up to something. That's for sure. But unless you want to march up there and confess in front of all these people, you might as well relax and wait to see what it is."

"Relax!" I squeaked. "How can I relax?"

"Try this." Chuckie stretched out under the tree, put his hands behind his head, and smiled contentedly up through the branches at the sky. "Is this a beautiful day or what?"

He peeked over at me when he said that, so he must've known there was a good chance I'd belt him in the gut or something. I didn't bother. I looked up at the bandstand. Buster had just introduced Mrs. Hildegarde, and she was

154

up at the podium, peering over her glasses at the crowd.

"You are privileged," she began, "privileged beyond belief to be a part of what is taking place here today. Enjoy. Enjoy and appreciate." She peered around for a while. "I am truly gratified to see a number of young people here among us. Let us hope that this will be for them the beginning of a lifelong appreciation of the arts. And let us be thankful that in Wakefield, at least, our young people have been given an opportunity to get out from behind their TV sets and truly discover the real meaning of the word 'art.' "

"*Behind* their TV sets?" Lymie said. "No wonder she doesn't like to watch TV."

That cracked Chuckie up. I don't think he realized that most times when Lymie says stuff like that, he's not even trying to be funny.

Mrs. Hildegarde said a few more things about how lucky we all were and then finished with, "Let us hope that this occasion will serve as the impetus for an artistic awakening in our community which will continue to grow until our town shines as an artistic beacon to communities everywhere." Which was probably her way of saying she'd be organizing a lot more poetry readings and stuff, but everybody seemed to like the speech quite a bit. Especially Buster. He was smiling from ear to ear. He even whacked her on the back as she headed toward her seat. She looked like she might bite his hand.

The fat critic was next. He stood there for a second, looking over the crowd with his sneery face. He was the first speaker who didn't look happy. At first I thought Buster had told him the news after all. No such luck. You could tell by the way he turned and looked at the heads. All of a sudden his face got all gentle and soft, like a mother looking at some sleeping baby. When he turned back to the crowd again, you could almost see him wince. You could tell he wasn't crazy about real live people.

"Those who don't understand fine art," he began, his eyes sweeping the whole crowd, "probably wonder how it is that we can be certain beyond a shadow of a doubt that these two works of art are authentic pieces of early Badoglian sculpture. And though viewing truly great art is, for the initiated, a visceral experience that does not lend itself easily to translation, I will try to explain."

"This I gotta hear," Chuckie said.

The fat critic turned and eyed the heads lovingly before continuing. "What is it that we see here before us today?" He let us think about that for a few seconds before going on, his voice growing softer and gentler as he continued. "In these rough-hewn stones, we see the Annunciation, we see the Presence . . . sketched out ruggedly, yet so illuminatingly. To the trained eye they contain an inner radiance, a glow of life if you will, a vision of creation itself." As he gazed down at the heads, Buster reached over and gave mine a pat. This time you really *could* see the fat critic wince. He took a deep breath and turned back to the microphone. "No, ladies and gentlemen, Badoglio did not betray his material. These stones do indeed have a soul."

The crowd really loved that. They must've clapped and whooped it up for two solid minutes. It kind of scared me. And it wasn't just the fact that I might get into serious trouble, although that was bad enough. It was something more, something bigger. I mean you spend your whole life listening to experts and figuring they know things that you don't. They're always telling you what's good for you to eat and what's bad for you to eat, or what's the best way to study, or how to solve disagreements without fighting (which I already tried out on Lymie and it didn't work). You can't even have an earthquake in California without some child-raising expert coming on the news and telling parents how they should talk to their kids about it so they'll still grow up normal. And if this art critic was any example of an expert . . . I don't know. It makes you stop and think.

"I *knew* those things were good!" Lymie said, and he kind of gave Chuckie this smug look.

"Hey, everybody!" Buster was yelling into the mike. "The Annunciation! Huh! What do you think about that?

What do you say, let's give this guy another hand!" He started clapping again like crazy and so did everybody else. Then some people in front stood up, and pretty soon everybody was on their feet.

Chuckie started laughing. "Look over there," he told us.

We looked where he was looking. I couldn't believe it. There they were, Mom and Mrs. Lawrence, standing up and clapping right along with everybody else. I felt bad because I knew why they were doing it. I'd watched enough nature shows on public TV to know that one of the laws of nature is that when a creature feels threatened, lots of times the first thing it'll do is try to hide by blending in with its surroundings. I couldn't see their faces, but I was pretty sure they looked like they were in shock.

I poked Chuckie. "This isn't funny," I said.

He patted me on the back and told me not to worry. Which was easier said than done.

Next we heard from the skinny critic. Being in front of a large crowd seemed to make him twitch even more than usual, and before he spoke he jerked his chin in so much he looked like he might be trying to swallow it. He called the heads "unequivocally Badoglian" and said only a master of Badoglio's caliber could "breathe a soul into mere stone." He told us the discovery was "a feast for Wakefield, a feast for the country, and a feast for art lovers everywhere."

His speech got a pretty good hand too, but nothing like what the fat guy got. I don't think he minded though. I think he was just glad the speech was over. He was still twitching and pulling in his jaw like mad when he sat in his seat again.

"What a day!" Buster yelled into the mike. "What a day, huh?" He stood there for a minute, shaking his head like he couldn't believe anything this good could be happening to him. "Hey," he continued, "we got a big day ahead of us, and I know you're all anxious to get on with it. But if you'll be patient for another minute, there's something I've been looking forward to sharing with all of you." He chuckled into the mike and shook his head some more.

I drew in a deep breath and held it. On the bandstand everybody but Buster looked like they'd just heard a fingernail scratching across a blackboard. You could tell nobody had given him permission to make any speeches on his own.

"You know," Buster said, "art's a pretty funny thing." He looked over at the heads. "Somebody like me sees something like these heads and thinks, 'Now those things are about as pitiful-looking as anything can get.'" He paused and turned back toward the crowd.

Everybody in the audience was looking at everybody else to see if he'd really said what they thought he said. The group on the stage looked like a freeze-frame of people watching a plane crash or something. For a second even the breeze seemed to hold its breath, and I could hear the sound of my own heart beating.

"Then we call these guys in . . ." Buster continued, jabbing his thumb toward the two critics, "and they tell us how these things are priceless works of art. They tell us that these things are not only beautiful, but that they have a soul. A soul, for crying out loud. And I wouldn't have made a doorstop out of them. That just goes to show what I know." He shook his head and kind of shrugged. "But if these guys are right, then in a way, it's kinda sad." He stopped and let everybody wonder about that for a minute. "Why sad? Because that would mean that these heads that we've come to realize are so beautiful and full of soul and what not, were made by a man whose days of chiseling valuable things like this are long gone. If I may be blunt, my friends, I refer to the fact that our dear friend Badoglio is dead. Deader than a doornail, last time anybody checked." Buster bowed his head and paused. "So what happens if we ever get tired of looking at our valuable heads here, huh? We're up sh . . . heh, heh . . . we're up the creek without a paddle, aren't we?" He shook his head sadly. "Kinda tragic, huh? I mean, as beautiful as we've been told these heads are, we're still bound to get sick of looking at them a few years down the road, wouldn't you

158

say?" He looked out over the crowd, which by now was really listening hard.

I took another breath. I think I was averaging about one every two minutes.

"Well, ladies and gentlemen," Buster said, "be sad no more. I got a little surprise for you." Smiling, he reached inside his coat, pulled out a big cigar, and lit it—all real slow to build up the tension.

I gulped and waited for the bomb to drop.

Buster puffed a few times and then studied the glowing end of his cigar. "With all due respect to our esteemed art *ex-spurts* . . ." He put a little extra oomph into the word "experts" and did kind of a bow toward them, at least as much of a bow as somebody as fat as Buster could do. "With all due respect to our *ex-spurts* here, I have to tell them, and I have to tell all you fine folks, that they've made a major blunder." He stopped and peered around from side to side and then leaned forward and spoke real low, like he was letting everybody in on something that was top secret. "You see, folks, these heads were no more made by Badoglio than my head was."

The crowd made one big gasp. The fat critic looked like he was thinking about having a stroke, and the skinny one looked like he might choke on his own chin. Mrs. Hildegarde reached for her heart, and the mayor and the council guys just sat there with their mouths hanging open. Buster's face was lit up like a Christmas tree.

"Heh, heh, heh," Buster said as he looked around and studied everybody's reaction. "That's right, folks. These things weren't made by our poor dead pal Badoglio. They were made by a couple of live people. And kids at that!" He puffed on his cigar and "heh-heh-ed" a few more times. "Old Buster here is proud to say he knows the real artists personally. We're real close as a matter of fact." He blew up another cloud of smoke. "You see, these kids—the real sculptors—were kind of upset about this whole thing and came to old Buster for advice, like a lot of the young people do. When they found out our *ex-spurts* here had

159

goofed and decided that these heads could only have been made by a master when really they were made by two kids who'd never even whittled a stick before . . . well, let's just say they were afraid of hurting the *ex-spurts'* feelings by owning up. Heh, heh, heh . . . but we don't need to worry about that. Nobody's feelings are going to get hurt. Hey, we all make mistakes . . ." He flashed a big smile at the critics. "Maybe not as stupid as the boner you guys pulled . . . but hey, we all do make mistakes." He looked back at the crowd. "And let's face it, folks. It could have been worse. Supposing some kid had dropped his Mr. Potato Head in the river. We mighta had that on display today instead."

Maybe it was the way the fat critic looked like he might explode all over the stage. Or maybe it was the way the skinny critic was working his face so hard that if you set him face down in the dirt, he'd've dug a tunnel. Whatever the reason, that was when the ice broke and just about everybody in the crowd started cracking up.

"Heh, heh, heh," Buster said when things had settled down enough so we could hear him again. "And we'd've all been here like a bunch of fools listening to speeches about Mr. Potato Head having a soul and giving us a vision of creation and what not. Heh, heh, heh. And we'd've had our police force here guarding an ugly plastic vegetable."

The two guys guarding the heads looked like their pants had just fallen down or something. Most everybody was laughing like crazy now, even Chuckie. He punched my arm. "I think you've got it made," he said. "That Buster really knows how to work a crowd."

Buster was up there beaming away, soaking up the laughter like a sponge. "Now I know you're all anxious to meet our young sculptors," he said finally, "but keep in mind how shy these artistic types can be, and give 'em plenty of room. Ladies and gentlemen, without further ado, I give you Wakefield's answer to Michelangelo and Leonardo da Vinci . . . and Grandma Moses . . . and you name it . . . I give you Tyler McAllister and Lymie Lawrence!" He poked his head out over the podium and looked right down at us

160

under our tree. "Come on, boys! Don't be shy! Get up and take a bow!"

Somehow my body stood up. I don't know how—I didn't tell it to. I looked over and saw Lymie standing there next to me. We both gawked at the crowd. The crowd gawked back. Only a few people clapped.

"Come on, folks!" Buster yelled. "Is that any way to treat a couple of artists? Let's hear it!"

A few more hands clapped, and then a couple of guys whistled, and before you knew it, you couldn't hear yourself think. I turned to see what kind of reaction we were getting from the bandstand and stuck my face smack-dab in the middle of that industrial-strength video camera.

"Smile, kid," the camera guy said.

My jaw dropped down so far the camera probably ended up looking at my tonsils.

19

I never did get to enter any sack races or dunk a fireman or anything. Neither did Lymie. Everybody had other plans for us.

First, Mom and Mrs. Lawrence came running over to where we were. Then Chuckie led all of us around, trying to find a place where we'd be free of reporters and crowds so we could think what to do. That problem got solved pretty fast when one of the guards for the heads came over and told us we were wanted for a meeting in the display trailer. Mom and Mrs. Lawrence started to come with us, but Chuckie told them it'd be crazy enough in there without extra people and that he'd take care of us. I was glad. Mom looked like her nerves were pretty well frayed, and Mrs. Lawrence was pacing around saying, "This is just the limit. You know that? This is *just* the limit." Chuckie gave Lymie and me a little push and we headed for the trailer.

"And what am I supposed to tell Lymie's father when he gets here?" Mrs. Lawrence yelled to us as we were leaving.

"Tell him his son's an artist," Chuckie yelled back.

*   *   *

The mayor, the whole town council, the two critics, Mrs. Hildegarde, and Buster were all in the trailer waiting for us, crammed in and stretched out along the viewing aisle in front of the real Badoglio stuff. They all kind of squished themselves to the side as we made our way down the line to the center of the group. Nobody looked too happy. Not even the exhibits.

The mayor ended up being closest to us, so he went first. Boy, was he steamed! "How dare you . . ." he snarled down at our faces, so close I knew he needed a breath mint. "How dare the two of you take it upon yourselves to bring shame on our entire town!"

"Hey, back off a little," Chuckie said, and pulled us in closer to him. "They didn't mean any harm. They're just kids."

"Yeah," Buster piped up from behind us. "And since when have you guys ever needed any help in bringing shame on the town?"

The mayor shot a nasty look at Buster but didn't say anything. Buster laughed.

Mrs. Hildegarde's face poked out from behind the mayor's. "Boys, I'm very disappointed in you," she said and shook her head. "Very disappointed. This was to have been a day of great joy for all of us. You've perpetrated a dreadful joke. Simply dreadful."

She looked so sad I really felt bad. Lymie and I hung our heads. There wasn't anything we could say to make her feel any better.

"Sorry," I said.

"Yeah," Lymie said.

"Hmmph," the mayor said. "There are situations where sorrow is not enough!"

Then everybody else on down the line had to give their two cents worth. Every once in a while somebody'd get so heated up Chuckie'd have to tell him he'd better settle down a little. I guess that kind of anger was to be expected. But the thing that kind of struck me funny, even while I was standing around shaking in my boots and getting yelled at, was that nobody ever doubted for a minute that *we* made the heads. I mean, if they'd found something that looked like the *Pietà* or the statue of David or something, and we said we'd made it, we'd've been laughed out of town. But when everybody took one more look at our heads, they just knew without even investigating any further that they'd been had. Except for the skinny critic. He kept saying over and over that the heads were "unequivocally Badoglian" until everybody, even the fat critic, told him to shut up. One council guy said to the skinny critic, "You're unequivocally an ass!"

"I'll buy that," Buster said.

After everybody got done yelling at us, the mayor started in again. "Boys, I don't know if you realize the serious consequences of your terrible joke. Do you realize that outside this trailer at this very moment there are a group of reporters waiting for us like a pack of wolves? And you can bet your bottom dollar they're loving every minute of this whole fiasco. They can't wait to rush back to their newspapers and TV stations to tell everybody how we've been made fools of."

"Heh, heh, heh," Buster said.

"I don't care about myself," the mayor continued. "I care only about the town . . ."

"Heh, heh, heh," Buster said.

The mayor closed his eyes and took a deep breath. "As the elected representative of this town, how in the world do you expect me to deal with that wolf pack?" He gestured toward the outside and stared down at us. "You tell me. What should I do?"

Lymie and I shuffled around and looked down at the floor.

"Well?" the mayor persisted. "I'm waiting. We're *all* waiting. You thought you were being so smart, now maybe you can tell us what to do."

Lymie and I looked at each other. Then Lymie looked

at the mayor and for once he spoke up without waiting for me to. "Laugh?" he said weakly.

The mayor winced. You could tell he wanted to back-hand Lymie pretty bad.

"You know, the kid's right," Buster said, and everybody turned to look at him. "Let's face it. You guys are going to look like fools no matter what you do. You can't change that. But now you got a choice. You can look like a bunch of puffed-up windbags that have been taken for a ride—which is what we all know you really are—or you can look like a bunch of good eggs who can take a joke. You know, if I was you guys—and I thank God every night that I'm not—I'd get out there and laugh my butt off, and I'd keep laughing my butt off until this whole thing blows over."

"Hmmph," the mayor snorted. "You go right ahead and laugh, Buster. But somebody has to protect the image of this town. Somebody has . . ."

"He's right," one of the council guys said.

The mayor cranked his head around impatiently. "What?"

"Buster's right," the guy said. "We have to act like we can take a joke. If we laugh, we don't look so bad. Hey, what do I know about art anyway? I run a hardware store."

"And I sell shoes," another guy said. "I'm no art expert."

It went on like this for a while, until one by one everybody but Mrs. Hildegarde and the two critics decided it'd be best to act like they thought the whole thing was a riot. And before they opened the door to meet the press and the public, some of them were already working on some practice chuckles.

I didn't get to say much of anything to anybody. As soon as I set foot outside the door, Mom snagged me and we took off. As we zipped by the bandstand trying to outrun the reporters Mom said were after us, I saw a bunch of people standing around looking at where our heads were. They were all laughing. When I looked down in front of them, I saw Lester Phillips sitting there with my head in

165

his lap. "Ty-wer's head is the best one," he was telling everybody.

Somewhere along the line Chuckie must've slipped Mom the keys to his car because that's where we ran to, which was a surprise in itself. Except for every once in a while when she used to drive Dad's Mercedes coupe, I'd never seen Mom drive anything but Volvos. She always said when you're carrying precious cargo (meaning me), you really want a car with a crash cage. My net worth must have plunged all of a sudden because after towing me across the park, she practically threw me into Chuckie's crash-cageless old Celica and patched out before I even got my seat belt fastened. This was a Mom I'd never seen before. I didn't even know she knew how to drive a stick.

Two minutes later we were sprinting up our front steps and locking the door behind us. That's when things really got strange. Mom was still leaning against the back of the front door like some kind of human barricade when it happened. She started laughing. And not just a little either. She laughed so hard she slid down the door and ended up sitting on the floor, and then she kept laughing some more.

I was pretty sure that this time I'd really done it. The week before I had her talking to herself, and now she'd gone over the edge. It kind of scared me.

"Mom," I said, "it's not that bad. You gotta pull yourself together." I reached my hand down to help her up.

Instead of standing up, she pulled me down so I was sitting next to her with my back to the door too. I stared at her. She was still laughing, but she seemed to have settled down some. Then the leftover laughter faded into a smile, and she put her arm around me and drew me in tight.

"Tyler," she said, "can you tell me *why* I bought this house and moved us here?"

I shrugged. "For me, mostly, I guess."

She nodded. "And why for you?"

166

"I don't know. You said you thought life in a small town would be good for me. More normal."

"Uh huh. And I wanted you to go to a regular school and do regular things around regular people. Am I right?"

"Yeah, you're right, Mom." I knew where she was leading, but I decided for once to go along with her anyway.

"Now correct me if I'm wrong, hon, but didn't we just get chased across the park by a pack of reporters?" She cocked an eyebrow at me.

I tried to smile. "I'll take your word for it, Mom. I was so busy running, I couldn't even see if they were really chasing us."

"I know reporters, Tyler. Believe me, they were chasing us."

Right then the doorbell rang. Mom and I looked at each other.

"I rest my case," she said.

The doorbell rang off and on for the rest of the day, and every time Mom would give me this look that said, "Would *you* like to handle this?" and every time my jaw would drop down and I'd shake my head no. It kind of scared me each time she did that. I'm not even that great at handling teachers and principals, let alone reporters. But I don't think she ever really planned on making me do it myself. It was just her way of reminding me about consequences, which she didn't need to do. In the last two weeks I felt like I'd learned enough about consequences to last me a lifetime.

Besides, Mom was a natural at that kind of thing. She'd open the door, smile, and say how sorry I was to have played such a trick, but that I had no idea it would ever have gone this far. And she had it timed so that when she got done delivering her spiel, that door was *closed*. It amazed me how smooth she was. A few reporters even managed to get their hands on our phone number, which was unlisted, and Mom handled them pretty much the same way. She'd talk to them as sweet as anything, but when she got done with what she was saying, they were talking to nothing but dial tone.

Before dinner I went up to my room and turned on my TV to watch the local news. As soon as the picture clicked on I saw the mayor. He was laughing away and saying how of course he had suspected foul play all along, but since the art critics had been so sure—well, who was he to go around expressing all kinds of doubts.

Then Lymie came on. I almost fell off my bed. Lymie isn't the kind of guy you expect to turn up on your TV screen. He was standing next to his father. And you could see Toddie and his brother Bart and Babette sneaking around behind them, waving at the camera. Plus I could see his sister with her arm going off the side of the screen, which I knew was attached to his mother.

"Me and Tyler never figured anybody'd think those things were real," Lymie said. "We figured they'd dredge 'em up and everybody would laugh, and they'd just chuck 'em back in the water." He shrugged and stared out from my set.

"It was wrong what the boys did," Lymie's father said, "but my wife and I were talking, and we gotta admit, it does make you stop and think. It really does."

Boy. Ever since I've known Lymie he's yelled at me to keep my mouth shut about everything so he wouldn't get in big trouble. And there he was having the time of his life being interviewed on TV. And his father was being all nice, and his mother didn't even rush on screen to belt him or anything.

And me, I end up hiding out in my house like some kind of a wanted criminal.

I didn't need to sit through any family meeting this time. Before dinner was even over, I'd practically signed my life away. I swore I'd never do another stupid (Mom's word was irresponsible) thing for as long as I lived. And I said if I had the slightest doubt about whether something I was planning was stupid, I'd check it out with Mom or Chuckie or my brother or some other responsible adult. I even promised that the responsible adult wouldn't be Buster.

And I wasn't just promising Mom these things. I was promising myself too. I knew that at the rate I was going, I'd probably end up getting an ulcer or having a heart attack or something before I was fourteen. My life-style was just too stressful. My old life-style, that is. In the future I planned on keeping everything open and aboveboard. No more sneaking around with secret plans.

I'd learned my lesson this time, once and for all.

20

Six weeks later they auctioned off our heads. Some guy from New York paid *five thousand dollars* for them! I couldn't believe it. They'd become collector's items already. And since they were sold as a set, I never did find out which one was worth more, mine or Lymie's.

The town council decided the money should go to buy new books and records and stuff for the Wakefield Library. Lymie was fit to be tied. He claimed the money was rightfully ours. I told him to drop it. For one thing, we were the ones who threw the heads away. And for another, I didn't want to go making waves with the mayor and the town council and Mrs. Hildegarde. Not to mention my mother. Sometimes I still catch her looking at me funny when I walk into the house, like I'm a hand grenade or something and she's checking to make sure the pin is still in.

I keep telling her she has nothing to worry about.

Lymie called today to say we've got a lawyer if we want one. This guy from Albany got Lymie's address out of the phone book and wrote him this big letter saying how we could recover not only the five thousand dollars, but a bunch extra for our pain and suffering. I recognized the guy's name. He has this ad on TV that says if you get injured on the job or run over by a car or something to give him a call. Lymie really wants to talk to him, but of course he wants *me* to make the call.

I still don't think it's such a great idea, but I'm starting to think—what's the harm in talking to the guy if it'll shut Lymie up. I haven't told Mom anything about it, or even my brother or Chuckie. No sense getting everybody riled up over nothing.